Ad

Dancing

"Whether you are doctor or patient, you see a bit of yourself in Dancing at the River's Edge. It demonstrates how profound the bond between doctor and patient can be—and how much power it imparts." —Susan Golick, Lupus patient and Founder, S.L.E. Lupus Foundation

"Living with a chronic disease is one of the most challenging experiences anyone can face. When physician and patient face this challenge together the bond they develop can actually be therapeutic in itself. This book is a testament to the healing power implied in this relationship."—Robert Wood Johnson IV, Chairman, Alliance for Lupus Research

"Dancing at the River's Edge is about the trials and tribulations of chronic disease...you won't be able to put it down once you pick it up." —Paul A. Volcker, former Chairman of the Federal Reserve under Presidents Jimmy Carter and Ronald Reagan

"Dancing at the River's Edge is a deeply personal exploration of feelings on both sides of the medical scene—the patient who suffers, hopes, and strives to retain her 'self'; and the physician who struggles to maintain a balance between knowing the truth while attempting to understand its implications. The authors draw the reader into their worlds in such a way that their own anguish, hope, frustration, searching, and mutual respect become the reader's emotions." —Virginia T. Ladd, President, American Autoimmune Related Diseases Association

"A book unlike any other; this slim volume probes the intricacies of a magical relationship, that of a patient with her doctor. Fortunately, this particular patient and this particular doctor are uniquely sensitive, perceptive, and articulate. The result is a heart-wrenching dialogue that carries profound and life-altering insights for us all." —Dr. David Sachar, Director, Henry B. Janowitz Division of Gastroenterology, Emeritus Clinical Professor of Medicine, Mount Sinai Medical School and Mount Sinai Hospital, and world's leading expert on Crohn's Disease

"Alida Brill and Dr. Michael Lockshin brilliantly illuminate the lonely path that the chronically ill person walks, providing fresh insights into the mind of both patient and doctor. A must-read for anyone who has traveled to the "other planet" that is chronic illness, or loves someone who is making this arduous journey...a life-affirming and deeply moving book."—Nancy Matsumoto, co-author of The Parents' Guide to Eating Disorders and freelance contributor to People, Time, Newsweek, Health, LA Times and The New York Times

DANCING AT THE RIVER'S EDGE:

A Patient and her Doctor Negotiate
Life with Chronic Illness

Alida Brill and Michael D. Lockshin, M.D.

schaffner
press

Tucson, Arizona

Cover and Book Design: Darci Slaten
Author Photos: Susan Contreras (of Alida Brill); Hospital for Special Surgery (of
Michael Lockshin)

The Publisher gratefully acknowledges the following for permission to reprint
excerpts from these published works:
from the Introduction by Sally Fitzgerald to *The Habit of Being: The Letters of
Flannery O'Connor,* Sally Fitzgerald, ed., courtesy of Farrar, Straus & Giroux, LLC,
NY © 1979; "The Precision of Pain and the Blurriness of Joy: The Touch of
Longing is Everywhere" in *Open Closed Open,* © 2000 by Yehuda Amichai, English
translation © 2000 by Chana Bloch and Chana Kronfeld, reprinted by permission
of Houghton Mifflin Harcourt Publishing Company.

First Paperback Edition
Printed in the United States
2010
Schaffner Press, Inc.
PO Box 41567
Tucson, AZ 85717
Copyright Registration Number: TXu-607-081

Contact Publisher for Library of Congress Cataloguing-in-Publication Data

For Michael, physician and friend,
with gratitude far beyond the words expressed in
this book, and for Jane, with admiration and love.

AB

To Jane (with apologies to
Nana Mouskouri, *La fille du soleil*):

Ne t'en vas pas,
Dessines-moi
Le chemin de la joie.
Nous marcherons
Jusqu'au *katun*
Ta main dans ma main.

MDL

DANCING AT THE RIVER'S EDGE:

A Patient and her Doctor Negotiate Life with Chronic Illness

Contents

Prologue

DANCING AT THE RIVER'S EDGE came about as the result of a series of colliding and random accidents, some happy and some otherwise. The idea of writing this book sprang, fortuitously, out of the close and enduring friendship between Alida (the patient), Michael (the doctor) and his wife Jane, and was conceived in the dining room of the doctor's house.

That we three came to know each other at all is due to the occurrence of a serious and stubborn autoimmune illness in Alida's life—the unhappy random accident that enabled the happier events to take place. A collision of that fate and geographical coincidence brought us together more than twenty-five years ago. Shared backgrounds and intellectual interests turned us into friends.

As this friendship grew we conversed about many things. We encountered surprises and connections, shared feelings and new thoughts. We talked about these over dinner; and Jane encouraged us to write these conversations down.

As we began to write, we explored some of our conversations in more depth and found that we were catching each other off guard. Each of us brought to light things we did not know about the other. We shared some secrets; we confessed to misunderstandings and mistakes; we learned to recognize, and to decipher, the complex coded dialogue, spoken and unspoken, that exists between an ill person and her doctor.

What you will read is a conversation, in places real dialogue—a changing of the attitudes by discussion and argument—in written form. This book is an intimate memoir about chronic illness, but a different one from those you usually see. It is a memoir that comes not from just one point of view but from the different sides of both doctor and patient.

We think of ourselves as collaborating cartographers, each charting a world we both know, but using different mapmaker's tools. We observe, take note, discuss, and learn from each other. Our conversation is often true dialogue—interaction, translation, comprehension, persuasion, compromise—those human qualities necessary to the success of any intense and intimate relationship.

In our conversations Michael has gained a deeper understanding of the particular coded language a patient speaks, or sometimes does not speak at all, but intimates only through non-verbal clues. And as a patient, Alida experienced, for the first time, the feeling of what it might be like to be in the heart and the mind of a doctor who must decipher this language, these unspoken concerns, and somehow move forward to arrive at a diagnosis and recommend appropriate treatment. As we wrote these conversational chapters, a friendship, already strong, became stronger by our renewed compassion for each other's roles and by our more personal understanding of the difficulties we each encounter when attempting to work at top speed under our individual constraints.

We like to think this book addresses serious issues in a way that offers support, comfort, and hope. We believe that *Dancing at the River's Edge* is relevant to the millions of people who are chronically ill, and for their families, friends, and caregivers. It has meaning for anyone who is living through a crisis that will not subside. This book explores the boundaries and shared experiences of a complex and intense interaction that has stayed stable through crises endured across decades. This book speaks to doctors, to patients, and to anyone who is in a role of helping or being helped.

In these pages we hope that caregivers will recognize humility, that givers of acute assistance will understand the transience of their actions in people's lives, and that those who are engaged in helping or being helped for long periods of time will learn the extraordinarily indirect but very readable ways in which both parties communicate their most secret fears.

Although the subject matter is serious, and at times we reach into the darkest sides of illness, we view this as an optimistic book about hope and dreams. In chronic illness there is an opportunity to reach for particular kinds of victory—triumph in the daily choice one makes to live as an individual demanding to be defined as someone other than, greater than, her disease. A tremendous victory lies in Alida's ability to reach past the illness to full personhood, and an equally important success for Michael to be able to see in Alida the individual beyond her chest x-ray and blood CRP.

We portray chronic illness through our separate and very distinct prisms. During the process of talking and writing, we learned that at some times our prisms were quite similar; at other times we found that we had each other wildly out of focus. At some junctures we found that our thoughts were either identical or mirror images.

We each have found our "weak spots" and our previously unacknowledged strengths in the choreographed teamwork required to keep a patient with serious chronic illness "up and running" as much as possible. This collaboration has been surprising, sobering, comforting, illuminating, startling, and truly collegial. Despite the inherently unequal power balance between a doctor and patient, our writing partnership has been one of equality and balance.

So, we embarked upon a collaboration to write just as we had collaborated through the years as doctor and patient. As we did so, we found that we intersected, we diverged, we came back together, we negotiated, and we compromised. As we each learned from the other, we found that, together, we could achieve more clarity than either of us had on our own. We now find ourselves seeing important issues in totally new ways.

We found optimism possible and logical. In the end we saw a story—one that reminds us of the unpredictability of our circumstances but that also reminds us to go forward, to negotiate, to communicate in pursuit of the dream of remission and cure.

— Alida Brill and Michael D. Lockshin

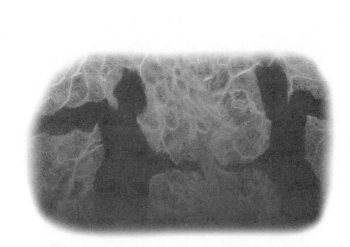

1

Measures of Time

It's easy to think about how to measure time—until you actually think about it. What scale should one use when measuring a human life? In the Western world our scales are linear and decimal. We speak about orders of magnitude, multiples of ten—tenths and ones and tens and hundreds and thousands. But a concept of 10 or 100 or 1000 or 10,000 days fits to no human scale and brings no universally recognizable image to mind. We do have concepts, like *decades* or *generations*, that describe the non-decimal pace of human life, but, lacking a biology-based scale of time, we tend not to think in these terms.

The ancient Mayans perceived time as a series of recurring cycles of periods within the human experience. To them a *kin* (pronounced k-e-e-n) was a day, *uinal* (pronounced we-e-n-al) twenty days, *tun* (pronounced t-oo-n) approximately one year, and *katun* (pronounced ka-t-oo-n), about twenty years. The world is renewed in a *baktun* (pronounced bok-t-oo-n) lasting four hundred years. On the scale of a *katun* people marry, achieve, see children grow, watch parents die, do or do not become disabled. The *katun* is the measure of time that describes the intersections of the otherwise separate worlds in which Alida and I live.

Biology and medicine have one scale for instant time, a nanosecond, a second, a minute or two—a fainting episode, a heart rhythm disturbance, a stroke, a convulsion, a sudden fall. One moment you are well, the next you are ill, never the other way around. This scale goes only in one direction: healing does not occur so fast.

Then there is the kind of time you measure with clocks, minutes and hours. This scale is bi-directional, pain or fever comes or goes, you come to the decision that you are or are not ill, that you will or will not call the doctor; the doctor decides that it is or is not necessary to act. A third scale, calendar time, measures time in months, seasons, and years: this new medicine is or is not going to work, you will or will not take that future trip, you will or will not attempt or achieve that future goal. Beyond that are the still longer periods that chroniclers know.

Time scales, for the most part, for most people, are irrelevant in day-to-day life. People interweave their different scales effortlessly, unconsciously, instinctively, rarely having to articulate and plan accordingly. The telephone rings, you answer—instant time. The business meeting takes place next week. Your child will graduate in three years. Determining such time scales is automatic. For most people it is almost unnatural actually to think about the many scales of time in which we operate out our lives.

But patients, unbelieving at first, grudgingly accepting later on, do begin to conceptualize greater, more abstract notions of time: instant, clock, and calendar, *kin, uinal, tun* and *katun*. If patients do not develop this construct, their doctors do it for them. This symptom, this pain, this fever is lethal! We deal with it now, in instant time! This other symptom, let's give it a few days, it probably is going to go away anyway, or let's try this simple thing to see if it works ("Take two aspirin and call me in the morning"), clock time. And the third thing, well, you can take that trip in September if we do this, but at such-and-such a cost in side effects or risk, or, if you stay here I can do something else, less cost and less risk—calendar time. Let's discuss it to see what is best for you. Decisions have to be made.

Decisions for the *katun* are hard, especially for the young. Plan A has a high success rate, you will soon be well, but the cost of that choice is that you will become infertile. With Plan B you won't have to take a leave of absence (or quit skiing, or not gain weight), but in twenty years you will be physically worse off than if you had chosen Plan A. Opting for relief on a clock or calendar scale carries with it a delayed cost that may not be seen until the next *katun*. Time scales must be articulated when choices are made.

Most books about being ill focus on short-term events; instead, this book speaks of a lifetime. What we have attempted to do is to look at how chronic illness transcends and transforms a person's life, from childhood, and early diagnosis, until the *katun* is unfurled completely and one's allotted time has elapsed. The lives of people like Alida are at times constrained and interrupted but are nonetheless fully lived.

The dialogue between doctor and patient is often asymmetric and is surely bizarre. It still seems surreal to me to discuss a twenty-year-old's pain today while, considering her options, I project in my mind the mother she will become a decade hence, the future grandmother in a *katun*, a grandmother whom, due to the disparity between her age and mine, I will never know. Beyond that, when the twenty-year-old is eighty, well, neither she nor I possess the clairvoyant powers that could inform such a guess.

And here is another absurdity: while my conversation with the patient transcends time, my frame of reference is within the instant. As I could not have predicted in medical school the emergence of the tools I use today, neither could I have known how badly flawed doctors' understanding of disease was in that archaic time. I cannot even begin to imagine what the doctors of the next *katun* will think about my advice for today, nor can I anticipate the tools the doctors of the next generation will use. So my patient and I stand frozen in this minute. I can only use the experience of the past to sketch out her medical future, all the while knowing that her future must remain unknowable to me.

MDL

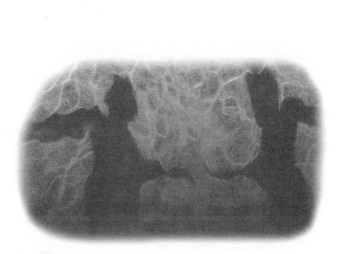

2

Two Journeys Begin

Something is Wrong with Me

There has been something wrong with me for most of my life. By that, I mean my health has been unstable for as long as I could comprehend the words, "unwell," "sickness," or "illness." I have a complex form of an autoimmune disease that decades after its early first warning signs appeared, still defies an absolutely clean and clear diagnosis. I no longer spend time thinking, or believing, that either a definitive diagnosis, or a cure, is likely to appear.

This is not the life I would have chosen for myself, but it is the life I have lived. Chronic disease is as much a part of me as my name. Yet, I fight against the notion that I am simply a walking, talking and breathing disease and not an individual independent of this condition. I push against the limitations and complications caused by its angry, inconvenient outbursts, and, even after all these years, I struggle against the reality that this illness is a primary component in my life. However, deep inside me, where self-deception is intolerable, I know it is an essential presence in my life, and will remain so.

I can't medicate, meditate, exercise, diet, or deny myself out of my medical status: I am a person with chronic illness. I sometimes choose to try any number of regimes I hope might alleviate some of the symptoms. Occurrences and episodes are unpredictable and vary in severity. One thing remains forever a constant—I am unable to wake up one morning and choose not to have chronic illness. There are no mental powers or psychological tricks available that will eliminate this fundamental truth.

However, I can and do make many other choices in my life. One choice I made years ago was more of a vow. I promised myself I would never write about the illness or my experiences as a patient. It was something I had no interest in doing. Since I am a writer, friends, colleagues, and editors asked me, "Why not?" Many of them offered suggestions as to how I might write a memoir or self-help book about the manner in which I have handled my situation and navigated my life's course. It was never a discussion that got past their first sentences. "No. I do not want to write about it, and I try not to talk about it, unless it proves necessary." My position on the subject was so adamant, and so widely known, that finally conversation about it stopped, with the exception of the occasional side remark, such as, "Well, it's really a shame that you are never going to write about it, because what you could say would be so…"

So, this is the book I was never going to write. Writing about being sick was an option that as a patient and as a writer, I would vehemently decline, out of concern for an individual's right of privacy. In a previous book, I wrote only two lines about being hospitalized, which I thought I had placed inconspicuously enough in a chapter dealing with issues of medical privacy. I came to regret those sentences almost immediately after the book was published. What has now changed my mind? Interestingly, it has less to do with the illness and its impact on my life. It is instead the result of a singularly unusual relationship in my life that I have had the great fortune to maintain for more than twenty-five years. It is a true friendship, but one in unique form—comprised of "doctor/patient"–"patient/doctor" exchanges over this entire period.

This reality forced me to face that there was more than one good reason to tell the story about a lifetime of being chronically ill. I have chosen to do this not because there is anything all that fascinating about me, or the form of my illness. I decided to write a book with this physician because in the midst of what could not be changed about my life, we were able to shake up some closely held stereotypes. Namely that a doctor and his patient chose to do something quite remarkable: we engaged in real and expansive conversations regarding the direction the disease was headed, treatment options, my life, and the larger and more significant issue of chronic disease itself—in terms both general and specific—over the course of almost three decades. During the long and capricious years of my illness, we have learned as much about what is wrong with me, as we have about the importance of what has transpired between us.

Michael will say that he did not choose to become a doctor of the chronically ill, that the career chose him. As someone who is chronically ill, one of the few choices I had been allowed was to select doctors, an option I exercised from a fairly young age. From my first meeting with Michael, my choosing to work with this doctor was the one option I understood might well represent a lucky throw of the dice. Over the years we have wrestled with many questions. We have agreed and disagreed; we have negotiated; we have had rocky moments in our passage together.

We have never given up on each other, or on the process. He has never given up on me. I have given into his wisdom, often, but not always, with reluctance. More importantly, he has allowed me the freedom to take some risks and chances that have enabled me to live a life, rather than merely to exist in a state of disease management. We have confronted issues of honesty and trust, control and power, denial and stubbornness, and a myriad of other things. Along the way, we also became close friends. I think it safe to say that during the long course of our relationship, we have both become better at helping each other become the best of what we are—patient and doctor engaged in a common struggle. I began by saying I would not have chosen this life.

Trust me: I will end my life thinking this. I can't, however, pretend that my condition has not shaped me or given me a set of perspectives different from ones I would have had, had I not been chronically ill. I insist, sometimes in anger, sometimes defensively, sometimes in cold fear, that I am not "it." Yet, "it" has also been a key ingredient in the mixture that has made me the kind of person I have become. "It" has influenced how I see the world and its inhabitants, how I enter the conversation as a person, how I interact with others, both those who are suffering, and those who have never had serious illness intrude upon them. In the final analysis, I confess, "it" hasn't been all bad.

AB

I Did Not Choose

I did not choose a career in chronic disease; this career chose me.

At about the time that Alida, an adolescent in California, first fell ill, I was an unformed and uninformed medical student in Massachusetts, learning about the very same symptoms she was enduring. At the same time that the youngster in a hospital bed on the West Coast was confronting the frightening reality of what was happening to her, I on the East Coast encountered my first patient with the same illness that Alida had.

I was disconcerted to witness confusion, if not fright, among my professors, in response to the symptoms of the sick young woman before their eyes. It was hard to believe. This young woman, at what should have been the happiest moment of her life, a few months pregnant with her first child, a few days ago well, was brought before us with a fever of 104 degrees, skin raw with the kind of rash that would frighten children at Halloween, hair rapidly falling out and almost gone, aching from head to toe, kidney function and blood cells dangerously abnormal, both her and her baby's lives suddenly threatened for reasons that she, and it seemed, we as well, could not comprehend.

Fate is too random for Alida's and my paths inevitably to have crossed—at that moment in time it was unlikely that we ever would meet—but, I fantasize sometimes that perhaps something of that California child channeled itself across the continent into the brain of an unfocused medical student in Boston and said, "This is the doctor you should become."

Back then, chronic disease had seemed to me rather dull. An exciting career, I thought, would entail diagnosing and curing a fast, decisive disease. A heart attack occurs. You die or not. Your appendix swells. A surgeon cuts it out. You are well. Cardiology, surgery—these are specialties that move fast, that conclude with clear results. If medical efforts fail, and if your patient dies, a pathologist will point to the dead part of the heart or the organ that burst inside and exclaim with certitude: "This is why your patient died!"

When I was a medical student, in the mid-twentieth century, medicine had new tools, deep knowledge of physiology, and certainty. Science was ascendant. Satellites were flying; we could head for the moon. An exciting career, I thought, would take root in the self-confident, definitive fields. Ask a question, any question at all, and, sure as the daffodils of spring, the answer would rise before your eyes.

Or not; illness did not always evolve so quickly and the signs could not be so easily read. When I saw that young woman during that first year of medical school, at about the time Alida first fell ill, I was surprised that her physicians did not manifest the confidence that, I had assumed, one could put on as easily as a white lab coat. After three or four weeks her organs failed and she was gone. In a mortality conference that week, and again in a class discussion a few weeks later, I asked what organ could have been fixed, what vital process had failed, in short, why had she died? My professors shrugged their shoulders and answered: "We don't know. They die."

Or not. This, my first experienced death, prompted a serious sortie into the medical school library. I learned that many patients with her illness did survive and that treatments, sometimes successful, did exist. I found great mystery (unexpected—it was such a confident age), so little was known about the abnormal processes of her disease; I found intimations of a new science that might engage the problem.

Thus my career direction changed, midwifed by mystery,

unsolved questions, new science, and curiosity, and perhaps by a little channeling from afar. I imagined that I could contribute to the science and that I would be able to intervene. My thoughts took place in the first person singular, active voice, in accelerated time. I act. Patient responds. The disease process may be slow, but knowledge would energize the clock. Intervention would be fast. Decisive.

I did not then understand—it took years to articulate—this: neither science nor interventions define the career that chose me. I could not learn this in the library and certainly would never learn this in the laboratory. Alida and her predecessors and her successors taught me, beat it into my head, again and again, that the core of a career in chronic illness lies in person-to-person interaction, emotion, adjustment, negotiation, choices, and evolution over time. Science and interventions are useful tools, but just tools. Like the separate DNA strands that wrap together at critical times, patients and doctors live parallel and occasionally intertwined lives. Neither fast nor decisive, we negotiate immediate, one, and forty-year goals, *kins* and *uinals* and *tuns* and *katuns*. We prioritize and choose.

My reward comes when a patient assumes control of her once disrupted life, my pain from knowledge that the optimistic youngster before me will not have the life she plans, and from seeing my twenty-first century tools—orders of magnitude better than those I thought sufficient long ago—fail. It is, of course, ego-affirming when on occasion I sort out seemingly unconnected signals to define a pattern of disease, understand how biological injury occurs, and target a specific treatment to repair a broken cellular cog. But it is much more joyful to know that, for this particular person, at this particular time, the disease is in retreat, and to be able to celebrate with this patient when normality returns.

Alida did not choose to be ill; I did not think that my career would evolve as it did. So be it. The nature of both our experiences is that our paths did cross and that we did develop and do now share a relationship that is unique in its intimacy and evolving over time. It is also a relationship that requires us both to maintain independent and separate ties to our other worlds, in order that the more important parts of our identities not be consumed by the chance events that led us to share these vital parts of our lives.

My career began. Alida fell ill. From these separate beginnings our mutual story evolves.

MDL

Suspicion, Witchcraft and the Magic of Dialogue

By the time I was about twelve years old, I had become a gambling girl. I knew how to work my personal odds. My body was betraying me, and nobody could figure out why. In defense, I thought it best to turn it into a secret betting game. On any given morning I would make a wager with myself: Would my legs work when I got out of bed or not? Would I run a high fever at night? Would I suddenly have swollen and hot hands or feet? Would intense pain shoot through me without warning? Would I look in the mirror and see a face disfigured, not by the ubiquitous acne of adolescence, but by some weird looking rash under my eyes? It was a game I would play with myself late at night, when I couldn't sleep for fear of what was coming next.

As I got older, I continued my addiction, but my wagers were now placed on the doctors. Physicians came in and out of my life faster than I could count them. On a night before a new doctor's appointment I would make a series of bets on him. (In those days, the doctors were always men.) Would this one be kind? Would he be gruff and talk to my parents and not to me? Would he think it was "all in my head"? Often, with my "luck," I would appear at the appointment with a new specialist on a day when there were no symptoms available for his perusal, therefore making a diagnosis more than challenging.

I remember nights when I "prayed" for an attack to come on by morning, so that I would be taken seriously. In those pre-feminist days of the early 1960s, adolescent girls' conditions were easily slotted into any number of loosely defined categories of "hysteria." Then there were weeks, or even months, when I was completely free of symptoms. My normal life would resume, which included athletics, especially running and basketball, and dance classes. During these times I would wonder if maybe I had been hallucinating—if it were not for the fevers, the swelling, the pain, the strange skin problems. The odds I feared most of all were the testing odds—what kinds of tests would the new doctor feel were required? How much would they hurt me or scare me?

By the time I had reached twenty-three, I had been in the hospital almost as many times as my age, and had probably undergone twice that many tests, of all varieties. I was jaded. I had abandoned my betting game. All bets were off because I had become a young woman who believed there wasn't a single doctor on the planet who knew what he was doing. Nothing amused me any longer. Self-preservation dictated that I replace fear with an unspoken rage. Frequently, I directed my feelings of angry frustration at the medical profession, and not at what was wrong with me. However, although I had been too strictly raised and far too polite and obedient to misbehave with doctors, no doubt there are one or two physicians out there who, if still alive, wish that they had never agreed to see me.

I was given gold shots. One traditional, but eccentric, older doctor, gave me a copper band to wear on my wrist, and of course, I swallowed pills that consisted of the full array of the latest anti-inflammatory medicines. A couple of them came complete with their own meta-diseases, including ulcers. Most upsetting was that omnipresent fallback strategy for control—the dreaded use of steroids. Nothing that I took or was subjected to did anything to stop the episodes of illness. Worse than that, none of the doctors, or sometimes teams of doctors, could figure out what it was they were trying to banish, other than the ghastly symptoms. As before, whatever it was would disappear, without leaving even a ghost of its presence. By this juncture in my life, I met every doctor, and each new recurrence, with complete suspicion.

Approaching thirty, I moved to Manhattan. I had decided to diagnose my own situation. I referred to it in my personal vernacular as The Rot. It was at a stage where it rarely disappeared, but instead took on wild and surprising new disguises.

This was the woman, with a wounded little girl very much present, albeit hiding inside, who, one late spring day, presented herself to Dr. Michael Lockshin. I surely wasn't betting on anything or anybody any longer. I was holding the winning "trifecta" ticket of chronic illness: I was desperately afraid, relentlessly stubborn, and in profound denial. I thought all that my life required was to get settled with a new doctor in Manhattan, the city I had decided to call home. Mostly, I was hoping against hope that the referral from my previous doctor would turn out to be a physician I could tolerate, at least marginally.

I have no idea what Michael saw when he first met me, or how much he remembers about our meeting. For me, the memory of that day is as clear as if it had happened yesterday. I even remember the dress I was wearing. In those days in Manhattan women breaking into new professional roles either wore the power-suit or the silk shirtwaist dress. I favored the shirtwaist dress. I chose to wear my best work dress. It was a black and white polka-dot silk dress; the top of the bodice was all white. I had on ivory tights and black flats with a bow on them. It was its own sort of uniform at that time.

There is no question that I had applied my make-up carefully; make-up has always been my defensive armor. And, of course, my hair would have been perfectly done. I am able to recall such details because I learned years before how important it was to make an excellent first impression on the doctor. It was essential to be absolutely and perfectly pulled together. Otherwise, there was always a chance he might decide you were crazy.

Michael D. Lockshin, M.D., came out to the waiting room to greet me, and immediately that was a telling new experience for me. I had always been accustomed to having a nurse, a receptionist, or an aide escort me back to see the doctor. Instead, this young man, who could have been an older brother, clearly not a father figure, came out to the waiting room. He spoke my name and then he shook my hand. He took me into his office first, not into the examining room. He asked me lots of questions, which was the usual routine. I quickly noticed, however, that not only did he seem to be listening to me; he also looked at me when I responded to his inquiries.

I lied about how I was feeling, and did so with my usual confidence, always fearing a sudden decision to hospitalize me for further exploration. However, this time when I lied, I had the sneaking suspicion my carefully well rehearsed, and often repeated performance, might not be all that persuasive to this doctor. At some point, he stopped asking medical questions, and asked me what I did. In other words, from the first moments of our relationship, he asked me about the person I was *within* and not the disease. I told him I was a researcher, which interested him considerably.

We diverted our conversation for a few moments to discuss my own work. I told him I had moved to New York to take a job at a social science research think-tank. I did not tell him that I had recently separated from my husband. Nor, did I tell him then that I felt I had to get away from my previous home in Berkeley, California because the pain of losing my marriage was far worse than being ill so often. I most certainly did not tell him then that I believed my husband had probably stopped loving me because of the disease.

I don't remember if he asked me if I had ever been married, though it must be that he did, and I have blocked the question from my memory. We had, by then, reached a point where I felt certain he might start to probe more intensely into my true feelings. I didn't know how I was going to waltz around my recent severe fever spikes at night. I had to keep him at bay—until I was sure of whether or not I was in a safe zone. But, just then, my eyes fell upon a framed article on his desk.

It was titled: *Witchcraft and lupus erythematosus,* by Richard Kirkpatrick, M.D.

Why was this article framed, why was it in his office, and what could it possibly mean? I scanned it as quickly as possible with one eye, while I kept the other on him. The article detailed the history of a young woman with lupus symptoms who was twenty-eight and suffering terribly—her prognosis was far from hopeful. She declined further treatment and returned to her birthplace—a remote village in the Philippines. There she was treated by the "witch doctor" of her native village and returned to normal health. I could not imagine what I would hear, but I knew I had to ask the question, "Why do you have this article on your desk?" I might have had an edge to my voice, my defenses and my defiance, barely, if at all, veiled.

He answered in declarative sentences. The importance of what he said has never left me: "I have it there to remind myself to be humble. This is a field where there aren't always obvious answers or solutions." However, it was the last thing he said to me which clinched it, then, and indeed, forever. He said the article reminded him, more than anything else, that patients often know a great deal about their own form of autoimmune illness and that doctors should listen carefully to their patients. I thought his professional field was my life's field and perhaps we might be in something together. My body and I were at war, and had been for a long time. Was I really hearing that this doctor was on the same side of the barricade, alongside me?

At that moment, most of my barriers dropped, and I asked him a simple question: "Will you please be my doctor?" I had never uttered those words in my life. Frankly, I remember feeling my heart pounding for fear that the answer would be he couldn't, or wouldn't, for whatever reason. Thank God, I have not had to say those words to anyone again. I don't remember his exact words but he made me understand that it would be his pleasure to be my doctor. I did not seem to represent a grim burden or obligation. I also sensed, correctly, he did not feel the main reason to take me on was to add to the ever expanding mountain range of tests results on the continuing expeditions to a diagnosis.

My memory of that first meeting was confirmed when I went back to a journal entry, and found these few telling words: *"I have never met a physician who thought that treating me or being in the presence of "my rot" would be a pleasure, but today I met MDL, and he said, it would be a pleasure to be my doctor. He did not say that finding the exact name for what it is matters as much as getting me to a better place than I have been. He saw me as Alida, not as Disease. I can't believe this has happened to me after all these years."*

Neither of us understood it at the time, but when he responded as he did about the article (which is still in his office), a true dialogue had begun. I ended our first meeting by confessing that I had been spiking high fevers at night for many months. I still don't know if he knew I had been lying in the initial moments of our meeting. I do know when I left his office I was beginning to think there might be a thing called a partnership between a doctor and a patient. And, maybe my careful personal recordings of the journey of my own disease made me, if not a medical doctor, at least somewhat of a lay expert about one patient—myself. I even dared to think, in my fantasy, it might be possible to be taken seriously not only for the professional work I did, but also for my observations about my own life lived with illness.

Through the many years since our initial meeting, I have come to take a far more compassionate view of the doctors who treated me before Michael Lockshin. With only one exception, they were all decent and good men, probably well trained, to the extent of the knowledge then available. They might well have been as frightened and confused by my disease as I was, but they could not let me see that. Perhaps it would have been more beneficial if they had been able to do so.

However, the core quality missing in all of those prior encounters was the one that would become the key to my later survival, both emotionally and physically. More than anything else what those earlier doctor-patient relationships lacked was what Daniel Yankelovich, the distinguished researcher and pollster, encapsulated in the title of his book, *The Magic of Dialogue.*

I would be a lying fool if I tried to convince myself, or you readers, that being ill from pre-adolescence until middle age is magical. I imagine treating legions of us with similar, and far worse conditions than mine, has been far from magical for Michael either. In the end, however, there is something that can happen when a patient and a doctor find they can move toward each other, if not as complete equals, then at least, as seekers, and not as judges. With this meeting of minds and hearts, something extraordinary occurs. It just might be a peculiar kind of magic.

AB

First Encounters

Long ago, at the time Alida became my patient, I would first meet new patients in a sort of garden patio with potted plants and windows overlooking the river, a comfortable, almost homey, reception area. My office had dark green walls and light oak furniture and obscure Mayan art for decoration. The bureaucracy has firmer control of the hospital's image now. The wall colors are a neutral pastel. The reception area no longer has a personality. Now nurses guide patients to the examination room.

I do not remember what Alida wore. I probably did not notice. Being male, I almost never do. I do recall noting that she was tall. Since I am rather short, I notice details like that. I also recall that she spoke forthrightly, analytically, and asked me to explain when I was vague. I like challenges; they keep my mind alert. Assumptions that can be questioned are assumptions that can be wrong. There was a bit of a juggling act, who will outwit the other? And underlying the bravado, I could see the secret fright of someone seriously ill.

I now meet new patients not in my office but in the examining room, which functions as a sort of wordless, inanimate partner in my practice. The room is small, about ten by twelve feet, sparsely furnished and unimaginatively painted in hospital off-white. It sits at the end of a long hall; the entrance is off-center to the left. A tall chair—easier to sit and rise if you are disabled—for the patient is along the left wall. It faces outward at an angle, allowing an easy glance out the open door. A guest in the chair to the right cannot see or be seen through the door. A second guest chair on the left faces the opposite wall. The patient and I, who have not seen each other before, can make eye contact when my footsteps are heard in the hall. I know little of what she already thinks, from the reception of my office staff, or the hospital, or the waiting room or those who were waiting there.

My first words are to her. If there are guests in the room, they bide their time. The way the door and chairs are set implicitly state: "This conversation is between you and me." The architecture protects her—and me—from letting others control what will soon be an intimate conversation between us.

In her opening comments I note her choice of words, her attitude, her body language, her relationship to the others in the room. The words of greeting and introduction, nonsense words establishing contact, perhaps an apology for lateness, perhaps a comment on weather or where she has traveled from, communication that is nearly automatic, almost non-verbal, taking just a few seconds or a minute or two, already tell me much. At this point neither of us has said a word about illness. We will get to symptoms soon enough.

I have my first impression. She is frightened or indifferent or angry, or not. She feels she has been coerced to come, believes that the visit is a waste of time, or not. Her spouse or relative or friend is supportive or hostile, or neither. With this patient I can be blunt, or not. With another my words will be very guarded, or not.

New patients are often well informed. They have seen other doctors, or have done searches on the Internet or have read brochures. Some throw a dictionary's worth of medical terms at me. I do not respond knowingly. I ask them to translate back to simple English. Medical definitions are too variable; prior conclusions based on presumed definitions are too often wrong.

Some conversations flow more smoothly than others. I

try not to be rushed, but my time is limited. I prefer to hear the story in the patient's words and in the order she decides. I learn about her priorities that way. But sometimes I must be direct, and interrupt. The story of an illness that begins, "It was two weeks before Easter, or maybe three. We were going to my sister's house in Connecticut. She was having a birthday party for her dog. It's a bichon. Her husband hates the dog…" will not get to the point we need to be, by the time I need to conclude. I am likely to interject, "And something happened on that trip?" The other type of story that does not work is, "I looked on the Internet and I'm sure I have lupus," and no details follow. This type of declaration will elicit from me, "Well, I would kind of like to make my own decision about that. Were there some symptoms that led you to think that you have lupus?"

In these first few minutes I usually do not know whether the problem is trivial or severe. On occasion, advance notes from other physicians have told me something; on other occasions a glance tells me what I need to know. But if the patient looks well it is not self-evident that there is no cause for alarm. Whether she is well or ill, most of this first visit will be spent in conversation, reassurance perhaps, or explanation of necessary next steps. Perhaps I will need to assuage terror ("People die from this, don't they?"), but more often I give the patient words she has never heard. I will likely introduce the concept of living with uncertainty, and I will try to shift focus from the near to the mid and long term. This latter point does not go easily with the very young.

Sometimes the new patient already knows a lot about her diagnosis. She may be changing physicians, seeking a different opinion, or seeking a cure when none exists. I have to introduce myself to her. I talk about the way I do things, outline what is negotiable and what is not, and listen to her version of the same. We don't always agree and patients don't always return. People who need no-gray-zone answers tend not to like my style. Those who do not accept negotiating treatment plans do not find happiness with me. I work best with those who reject, argue, suggest, challenge, innovate— those who partner in their care, who accept that we are in this together, and concur that our defeats and our victories will be shared.

I do not know what a young woman thinks when she first intuits that she may be unwell and that she needs to seek advice. Those private and personal moments are rarely discussed with me. I imagine the thought "I am sick" comes as a surprise. Perhaps the first hint was fever, a common flu, perhaps, and then something more. Or a routine activity caused unpredicted fatigue. A rash might have been allergy, then not. Joint pains are sprains or injuries; they do not go away.

Yesterday, life was normal and now it is not. Most new patients have discussed the symptom with family or friends, who may have been dismissive or appropriately or excessively concerned. It usually takes weeks to arrive at the "I am sick" conclusion, and still more time before a would-be patient makes the first telephone call. And still more time to the appointment.

Newly ill patients tend to come with one of two ideas about what they have. If an acquaintance, a relative, a friend, has or had a horrible disease, or if she reads or watches television, has searched the Internet, or has a vivid imagination, some devastating illness has come to mind. The other attitude is that this is a simple thing for which the doctor will give a prescription, and, not to worry, all will soon be well. Each patient holds different mindsets, different fears, and different potential responses to my opinion and proffered plans.

Both the patient and I have goals for this first meeting. Mine are to establish, with reasonable dispatch, a working diagnosis and a diagnostic and treatment plan. I don't intuit the patients' goals; I ask. Certainly one of her goals will be to figure out who I am. I assume—I know—she is judging me. She may have come with a printout from our web site or some public document that carries my CV.

It is true that doctors obfuscate. *Iatrogenic impulse* is a mélange of Greek and Latin that in simple English means: "Why did you come here today?" This is my usual first question to the patient. What specific symptoms, what specific alarm, led to the call for an appointment, at this time, not a month ago, or not three months hence? Although I think the question obvious, it often surprises new patients. Some think I am joking or that I have insulted them ("To see you, of course"). But the question is serious. I don't give up; I ask it again.

The answer tells me about the patient's priorities and about her state of mind. It may be fear, or it may be pain. It may be that a television program or print article said something that matched a symptom. Sometimes a family member insisted that they come. Sometimes another doctor found an abnormal blood test on a routine examination. The answer tells me what she expects me to do.

Some answers are very indirect. The patient may think—but not admit—that her symptoms point to an underlying and rapidly fatal cancer. I often don't learn this until I ask, toward the end of the interview, "Is there something else you would like to ask? Is there something else that is bothering you?" I learn amazing things. Diagnoses that are fantastic or sometimes quite inspired, and family issues, and other seemingly irrelevant things rise to the fore.

Mostly it does not take much time to develop a working

diagnosis. If I see a swollen hand or note a rash, or detect hair loss, even before I have heard the first several sentences of the patient's story, I likely have an idea of the cause already in mind.

At this point asymmetry in our dialogue occurs. I have a fairly good idea about what the future holds, but most of the time she does not. Diagnosis implies prognosis, so I begin to think of things it may not be prudent to tell her at this time. I think about what happens to eighteen-year-olds who take the medication I am going to prescribe: weight gain of forty pounds, acne, and a face so round that her close friends will not recognize her on the street.

I think of young women who cry when others shun them because they fear contact with a contagious disease. I think about youngsters deserted by their friends when they fall ill, or loved ones and spouses who declare, "I can't take it any more," or a supervisor who fires a person who is unwell. I also know that unexpected hospitalizations disrupt lives, that impossible pregnancies destroy relationships, and that invisible pain and fatigue are inexplicable to disbelieving friends and kin.

I also know that these things may not, probably will not, happen to the young person sitting opposite me. I know that most likely very few of these bad things have come to her mind. So I accept the asymmetry in this conversation and keep to myself what I surmise but she does not. Instead I stay on the pragmatic plane: "Here is what we are going to do," I say. I do not elaborate on what she may not know.

She and I will deal with the other things at a more opportune time. Not now. Not on the day that we first meet. I hope that my eyes do not betray my fears.

MDL

Childhood of a Different Place

There is a large waiting room. It is a common one for the patients of all doctors who are working with Michael. I call it the "waiting pen."

I think of it as the waiting pen and not the waiting room during those times when I am in a personal winter's moment. At other times, it looks like just what it is—a large nondescript room with old, almost ancient, magazines and lots of brochures about the illness you have, and those you don't have, but the person sitting next to you probably does.

At other times it feels more like a corral. There you sit, waiting your turn to be called for slaughter. For me, "slaughter" means yet another diagnosis, or a new preliminary diagnosis, an upsetting or grim prognosis, the order for the next series of invasive tests, the as-yet-untried drug treatment strategy, conversation about clinical trial risks, or, worst of all, a nonnegotiable decision to hospitalize immediately.

Not surprisingly, the room feels most like a pen when it is filled with people far sicker than I am, at least for the time being. That is when I utter what passes for my silent prayer that all the other patients be protected from further harm. And, then, I add an extra one to all the gods, familiar and unknown, near and distant, to keep me far away from the place those suffering through severe and advanced stages have reached.

When I arrive at the pen and find there are children beset by memories, I become restless, and anxiety instantly gets the best of me. I can't help myself. I look at the children, but try hard to avoid their direct gaze. Inside my woman's body a war is being waged. The child I once was wins the battle quickly and without much struggle from the woman I have become.

It is the child-woman in me who wants to go over to one of them, or each of them, and say: "Look at me. Don't you think I look pretty good? Well, I want to tell you something very important. By your standards, I suspect you think I am rather old. But, I've had this bad stuff, just like you, from the time I was your age. Here is what you need to do: you need to go on and on, and 'keep on keeping on' and never give up. Do not forget your hopes for the future. Do not let anyone take your dreams away from you or talk you out of them."

I want the mere fact of my existence to give them courage. I don't say a word, of course, because it would be inappropriate on every level to approach an unknown and unwell child. I don't know their diagnosis. And, I don't know how sick they are. I do not know if they will reach adulthood, and more than likely, they don't either. However, if they are at least twelve, they have probably already thought about all this over and over.

The true reason that keeps me from engaging in even fantasy conversations with the children in the pen is due to a secret I have always kept hidden deep inside myself: I'm not always sure its been worth the effort to continue this challenging dance with disease for an entire lifetime, where no matter what I do, at least a part of me is constantly defined by illness. How would a child react, knowing that I, and millions of others, at times feel our lives are only about the fighting on and on and on, until it finally ends?

How would a child of twelve or fourteen respond were she to meet a grown woman such as myself, and discover that, from her point on in life, until she has reached my age, she might well be spending a huge amount of her time in the hands of the medical profession? It is because I am not always sure myself about the efforts of this journey that I silence myself, not merely out of respect for decorum and privacy.

Children who are chronically unwell tend to be, if not omniscient, at the very least keenly observant. These children, quiet and wise, can often discern who is lying and who is not. Chronically ill children sense the confusion, frustration and fear in other children and adults, without needing explanations. They possess comprehension of such matters far beyond their years. They see these emotions in the eyes of their friends, teachers, family members, mothers and fathers, and in their doctors' eyes as well. I know this because I have lived this life. I have been an earlier pilgrim, on their path, blazing a trail from its beginning stages. They are unwittingly following in my footsteps.

If I had known when I was only twelve, as this expedition toward diagnostic discovery was just beginning, that by middle age my entire life would be defined as much by my health crises as my life markers—friendships, marriage, a milestone age, great loves, career, travel—if I had known then that all these things, and many more—would always be balanced against multiple hospitalizations, seemingly endless steroid rotations, surgery, lung scans (invasive and not), brain scans, years on an anti-leukemia drug, violent and toxic drug reactions, experimental drugs, chemo-therapy infusions, loss of my hair (more than once), and so forth and so on— if I had known at that young age that there also would be the sweetest interruption of all, a full respite from disease, known as remission, and that it would be seized from me suddenly by the sneak-mugging of a robust recurrence of illness—If I had known all these things—what exactly would the child Alida have thought about going forward into this kind of life?

How would I, aged twelve or thirteen or fourteen have reacted? What would I have done, if I had been told I would never be completely well, and never totally free of the worry of the severity of the illness when it returned? What would I have done with this bluntly stated factual information? "This will not go away. However, you might live to be quite old and it will scar your personal life in ways that you can neither understand nor contemplate at your young age. No matter how hard you try, this illness will disrupt your plans, change your daily schedule and your life's patterns. It will even invade your dreams." I shudder to think what my reaction would have been had I been given that knowledge early on in my life.

One afternoon, I watched a girl sitting across the room from me. She was working diligently on a school assignment, an attempt to close out her surroundings. I know that trick. I wanted to say to that particular little girl, who could barely struggle into the tall seat (the only empty chair left), as she immediately pulled out her schoolwork, "Look, this thing that has happened to us, it's more like a place than a medical condition. It's a place where we live, and others do not. I think it absolutely stinks, and frankly, in my opinion, you should give yourself permission to be as angry as you want to be that all of this is happening to you. I have never been able to express this, so maybe extreme anger will help you. Give it a try."

I did not say this or anything else because it would be as unethical an act I can think of to perpetrate on a child. In any event, resorting to anger is probably as useless an act as giving up chocolate or not eating wheat, or anything with yeast, or swearing off dairy products, or drinking gallons of some expensive green slime to boost the immune system, or any of the other legions of diversionary activities I have engaged in over the years.

Maybe, it's best not to say anything to this girl, with her pencil and her homework, just in case it turns out that in her lifetime cures will be found. Somewhere and everywhere, researchers are, step by step, one patient study at a time, perhaps even one case at a time, unlocking the code to understand what makes our systems decide to transform us into a moveable feast and devote a lifetime of apparent enjoyment devouring our tissues, our bones, our vital organs. Perhaps, from a definitive understanding of the code gone awry, these research doctors and their scientific colleagues will come forward with a new translation of the meaning of these diseases, resulting in real treatments, ones that end more suffering than they create. And maybe, just maybe, this girl's future holds the ultimate victory, the one we all dream about—doctors, and patients of every age— that eventually there will be the total curtailment of this phenomenon known as autoimmune disease.

I do not believe in Santa Claus, The Easter Bunny or Tinker Bell, nor have I ever witnessed Elijah sip from his cup at the Seder table, but I still dream a cure will be found for the entire array of these diseases that gnaw away at our interior landscape. Personally, the dream does not matter that much for me any longer. I have sustained too much collateral damage from the disease and the drugs, to say nothing of the irreparable psychic damage, for a full cure to be of all that much benefit to me at this point. My dreams, indeed, all my hopes, are aimed at the youngsters.

As I finally hear my name called, and walk back into the hallway of the examining rooms to learn my own verdict, my thoughts are directed at that young girl doing her homework, and all the others she represents, in my own country, and around the world, who are just beginning to comprehend they are citizens with dual residency—in the kingdom of childhood and in the land of the chronically ill.

The one thing I do know with certainty is that those

kids sitting in the pen who are waiting for a new verdict or a confirmed one, will not be subjected to what I was at their ages. There is far more awareness in today's world about disease and illness. Although children can still be quite cruel to those who are different, it is no longer an acceptable form of playground conversation. I trust that today's children will not be the subject of ridicule and bad jokes that I endured, like most of my generation, no doubt. What remains is that they will also find any number of things they will not be permitted to do, because they can't or because it is not a wise idea. I remember still with stinging regret that I was never able to go on overnight camping trips with my school or Girl Scout troop. Only once did I experience sleep-away camp, and then only because my mother signed on as a parent-counselor, which was hardly the point for me.

I am certain however that these children will not have to face the kinds of doctors I had to deal with, and will not be subjected to the same primitive and raw drug experimentation or be subjected to trials by a variety of medical grand inquisitors that I endured. The invention of the MRI removes a variety of truly hair-raising and painful tests these children will not need to undergo. Doctors still need to search for answers, but modern technology makes it less likely these children will feel like a combination of lab-rats and guinea pigs. Medicine as a profession has advanced, and the manner in which doctors come into the world as physicians, mercifully has changed dramatically in the years since I was an unwell girl.

For the healthy, childhood is a time of discovery, of testing limits, real and imagined—defining one's own turf, whether it's the locked teenage girl's diary, a boy's clubhouse, a dollhouse, or a tent in the backyard. It is a time of make-believe, pretend and fantasy, all mixed in with childhood versions of reality, for exploration of new worlds, internal and external. But, for the child who is entering into a journey of discovering what it is like to have a life accompanied by an unwanted intruder, it is also the time for taking those first steps down the road of acceptance.

For those children who do not enjoy full health, their experiences are less about discovering new adventures than about learning what they will be unable or forbidden to do. For us, childhood is a place of the exploration of our bodies as battle stations, not play-stations. When I think back on the life I have lived, it is the experience of my childhood, not the later and far more life-threatening adult dramas, which still gives me nightmares on a regular basis.

When I enter the darkest portion of an episode of illness, I remember the child I was and take comfort that I will never have to go through that again. So it is, sometimes, when I see an individual child in the pen, that I wish for all the world I could hold this child in my arms for a moment and say, "Come with me, I'll show you the way through this. It won't be so bad, if you just stick close to me." I can't and I would not, but it is what I feel when I look at the children, because I think I can read at least some of their stories. I only have to look into their eyes.

I believe I can read their eyes in a way that even their very sensitive doctors or loving parents are unable to. I can read in them a particular psychic exhaustion mixed with fear, determination, and despair. In some of these faces, I see a subtle look of resignation; these are the children who have already begun to lower the bar of life's expectations. It is hard to explain in words what it is I see. There is no external form of expression of what this feels like for a child. Words can't describe what it is like to be inside the child who knows before she has reached adolescence, or just as she approaches it, that she has already quietly and privately adjusted her expectations—she already understands there are many things which are normal for her friends but that are unthinkable for her, and that other things, as well, will forever remain unattainable.

Her desires and her dreams might well be trumped by the reality of her illness. I can see it in the eyes of these girls—these girls who see and understand, both too much, and too little.

By the time I was a teenager, I knew there were activities and experiences already marked "off limits" for me. Now, when I read that unmistakable look in a child's eyes, I usually walk down the hall, to the women's restroom, and try to pull it together. It is not in sorrow from the memory of what I was. Instead, it is that I need a moment to release my utter grief about what that girl might be thinking about her own life, as she waits to be called into the examination room. As I stand in front of the mirror in the women's room, I see more than just the image of my mature woman's face. In the reflection, I see again with complete clarity, the little girl I once was—terrified, totally confused, but also resolved to be brave, and never to cry.

When I see a child who I know is in horrible physical pain attempting also to be so brave, and not let her agony show to her obviously distraught parents, I can see myself at that age doing the same thing. I think then how little has changed in more than four decades. Childhood and chronic disease are a toxic mixture of disappointment and false maturity. Inside a child's brain lies the understanding of who should be protected from the truth and who should be told the truth. We understand too early we are not like other children. When we are permitted to live solely as children, if at all, we live in a parallel sphere. If we are smart or curious, we want to know perhaps more about our disease than we are able to process emotionally.

Doctors like Michael must watch and listen and judge what is really going on inside that child's body and mind— to the extent they can fathom a child's unspoken thoughts and feelings—and make their own internal calculations about truth and knowledge. How much should a child know about her likely future, or even the next few years? Should a child be denied the right to know as much as she can comprehend? Should she be told that this field of medicine changes constantly and there is reason to hope her disease can be controlled, or at least managed to the point where it really is no longer a daily presence in her life? And, would that be the truth? Or, if not the absolute truth, would it be the right truth for that particular girl, in that particular moment in her life, in that doctor's examining room? Who is the ultimate judge?

The ugly game of being ill as a child isn't the only game we can play. Chronic illness, even when it begins in childhood, can be sidelined, or "benched" by joys that can take the center stage of childhood, at least for a time. There is the excitement and triumph of artistic or academic achievements, and of many other experiences that are not about the disease. If you put your mind to it, you can have these other things coalesce into something called a childhood.

Yet, the haunting question never leaves me for very long. How much do these children need to know about how dark and difficult their lives might become later, when youthful days have already been irrevocably disrupted by the diseases inside them? Throughout my own childhood, I was convinced one day I would wake up and "it" would be gone forever, vanished into thin air. I don't know if I want the children I observe in the pen to hold onto this dream, if it is to be as elusive and ultimately impossible, as it has been for me. However, I also trust these children of the 21st century will have a life that diverges significantly from mine. I dream that whatever is discovered to treat chronic autoimmune disease more effectively will be in time to alter their childhood—if not erase the pain they have already suffered, at least mitigate the memory of its wounding power.

At the end of all my speculation about what I might or might not say, if it were appropriate to say anything at all to the children in the pen, it would be only one thing: I would tell them it is not their fault. They are not to blame for what is happening to them. We don't know why it happens, but it is not something they have done wrong that has caused this to happen to their body, and to their lives.

My predominant memory of a childhood divided by and interrupted with illness, is that I so believed it was really all my fault. I do not believe I am alone in this sentiment. It is one of the reasons I have become, as an adult, quite hostile to the "body-mind" movement in alternative health care. The theory that states, "Happy people don't get cancer," or, "People who are in touch with their feelings do not have chronic illness." These are literally hundreds of variations on a comment directed at me quite frequently: "If your body is attacking itself, surely you must be unable to handle something in your life."

I am usually polite, unless I am up against a true zealot, and then I am quite likely to say, "It is the disease my body can't handle. Want to give this a try, and see how well you do at it?" While I know there are those who believe deeply in the power of alternative medicine, and I have not been a total stranger to its songs of seduction, for me it smacks too loudly of a harmful refrain: "blame the victim."

Diagnosis and understanding the course of autoimmune illness remains an elusive part of medicine; therefore, a child, who understands only the basic concept of a body that is not behaving itself, is hard-pressed not to take that inevitable next step into self-blame. A chronically ill child often "upsets" the family's plans, routines, and the normal activities of the other members of the household. It's quite easy to blame yourself when you see what your illness does to the way your family and your home functions.

You have sporadic symptoms, mixed symptoms, and the game is on—the game is that you, the ill child, is seemingly in control of an entire household, whereas in fact, the child feels like a run-away car that careens from diagnosis and treatment possibility to crisis, to hospitalization, but it's a vehicle that has no brakes.

An ill child is likely to get more attention than a well child. Siblings are jealous, and the unwell child is ashamed and must defend herself against accusations of being overly dramatic, or attempting to capture all of the available adult time and attention.

I can recall experiencing lovely moments as a girl, but I understood them as vacations from my real childhood. My girlhood was in a different place, a place called, "She's Ill. Again." While we appear to occupy the same spaces and places as the well children, our interior lives are different, and, so too are our experiences with the medical world. The average child sees a doctor once or twice a year, unless there is a crisis.

For us, doctors' appointments are as much a part of our rhythms as seeing teachers, classmates, families, or doing homework assignments. Seeing the doctor or teams of doctors is an ever-present fear as well as a reality. It is terrain unknown to a healthy child. It is truly "another planet," a metaphor whose significance I would only come to understand fully at middle age, with both resignation and sorrow.

To the extent possible, doctors, parents and everyone who plays a role in a sick child's life must attempt to become not inhabitants, but at least cartographers, of this "alien" planet. Until the rockets of medicine and science are developed and built which will deliver all children from this planet of chronic illness, something can be done now to alleviate some of the suffering. The profoundly damaging suffering caused by feelings of isolation and "otherness" can be reduced significantly if the chronically ill child does not also feel as if she were an alien being. Fortunately, that is something, that, with enough education, collaboration, conversation, and dialogue, we can attain, even before the dream of cure is realized and fulfilled.

AB

Adjust, Educate, Collaborate

Once I have taken the history and completed the exam, I like the next part of the interview to take place in my office, in a room that reflects my taste to some degree. I invite the patient and those with her to join me for a conversation. If she comes with a big family, I have to ask some of her loved ones to wait outside.

The green walls and the light oak furniture are long gone. The hospital, wanting to set a single tone, now controls the overall design. Although it dictated the furniture and the paint, the wall and shelf decorations are still mine. I still have the Mayan art. The framed article about witchcraft remains.

Two chairs face me across a cluttered desk. I used to have a couch and a chair next to that so I could talk to the patient without an interposing desk, but this is New York in the 21st century, we make living rooms out of what mid-Westerners call closets, and my office nowadays is small. One desk and its chair, two seats on the opposite side, a third sometimes stolen from my secretary's desk and squeezed in as well. A fire marshal's nightmare, but more comfortable than a discussion in the examining room, with rumpled sheets, discarded gowns, and medical instruments scattered about.

The design is otherwise conventional: diplomas to the patient's right; books, telephone, computer screen with a mysterious screensaver behind my back; X-ray viewing box, some personal pictures, another computer screen (and a clock) visible only to me. At midday, remnants of lunch may be seen (or smelled).

Having dressed and gathered her clan, the patient comes in, and I am usually busily completing her chart or reading laboratory studies or urgent mail. I look up when they enter.

Instinct and a New England upbringing tell me that I should stand, but, space for my chair being tight, I usually muster an awkward half-rise before they sit down.

At this moment I am in control of the conversation—it is *aequanimitas* time, this term coined by Sir William Osler, the great nineteenth century physician who left, among his many gifts to posterity, an instructional booklet for beginning medical students, the title of which is the Latin word for *equanimity*. Always appear calm, Osler warns. A physician's arrival into a chaotic scene is calming for those frightened by disease; however, if you display fear, it will be instantly transmitted to all. So I self-consciously adopt Osler's admonition to young doctors always to appear calm—as I set the tone of the conversation, devise a plan, keep hope alive. I know my role.

Most likely she does not know hers. She has not known chronic illness before, and this is still all new territory for her. She may be terrified by—or unaware of—the fact that her life has just changed. She probably cannot anticipate the next steps, but I have seen them before.

I know the timeframe, the difference between the *kin* and the *katun*; almost certainly she has a different timeframe in mind. Others in her life, and she as well, have expectations. Perhaps she wants as a first priority for pain to go away. Or for fright to be resolved. Or just to feel normal again. She will have many needs. I will anticipate some but will find others to be a complete surprise.

We will need to use the same metaphorical language. I will describe a battle, a detour, a bump in the road, a challenge. The foe will be sneaky, unfair, sometimes merely a nuisance, indefatigable, but never beyond our ken. The patient and I will have to have similar goals.

A fifteen-year-old is not a thirty-year-old is not a sixty-year-old. A person with five children differs from a new college graduate seeking a first job. Rich or poor, immigrant or native-born, black or white, young or old, I will mostly converse in what I hope is her language, not the other way around. Otherwise we will talk past each other and fail to understand.

When she walks through the consulting room door I have not planned what I will say. During the initial history and examination I gleaned an intimation of what she may wish to hear. Her body language and her eyes now tell me more. Almost always I speak first, and almost always I begin with direct speech and with good news. My first words target (what I surmise is) the major fear. "Well, I don't think it's lupus," I might say, or "I think we have a way of dealing with this," or "I don't think you are very sick." Sometimes it is, "Yes, you will see your kids grow up," or, "Just to be clear, I intend to dance at your wedding." Every now and again I have no idea what the patient fears, and I may begin, "Why don't you tell me what you think is wrong?" or "What would you like me to do?"

The questions may bring out the things she has not yet talked about: the Internet printouts, the aunt who had brain cancer, the cousin who died horribly of some inconceivable disease. It's easier to deal with these straight out, preferably with "No, that's not what you have," but, if needs be, with "Yes, but you are a very different person, and this is a very different year."

From this point I adjust the conversation according to my best guess. I can use one vocabulary for the scientifically well informed and another for the untrained. I can choose to discuss the gray zones of medical thought ("Maybe this, maybe that") to those who intellectualize or are comfortable with ambiguity or I can display a degree of certainty ("This is what it is") that

I may not actually feel. I may defend my diagnostic thoughts against those of other physicians at famous clinics, whom she saw before she came here, whose skills I may know, or we may talk of curanderos or Chinese herbs. (Everyone asks about diet; everyone asks about stress.) Doctors think of this kind of adjustment of conversational modes as mandatory flexibility. I think of it as a sort of game. To give the same message, but make the same point in different ways helps to keep my mind active, and livens up a day.

Adjusting to a patient's style is guesswork that can sometimes go very wrong. I was once discussing with a young woman her severe (but ultimately very hopeful) prognosis and my plan—it was not a new diagnosis. The visit was a second opinion consultation; she had heard the message before—I saw tears fill her eyes. I reacted as I usually do: confront the fear head-on to neutralize. I asked her what thoughts had elicited her tears.

"Why am I crying?" she asked. "Because you just told me my life is over." I said that she had vastly overestimated the grimness of what I had said and that she would, in fact, do quite well. Years later I learned that she thought my question had been scornful and patronizing. She hadn't said so then.

It took similar miscommunications and many years for me to learn to say right away, "It's not cancer," or "You are not in trouble," or to preface a question about a false positive test for syphilis (an important diagnostic clue) with, "This is going to sound really strange to you," or "The question I'm going to ask doesn't mean what you think," because most new patients don't volunteer some of their secret dreads.

There is style to communication and there is content as well. I'm flexible with the former but more rigid with the latter. At this first visit I need to achieve these goals: form a working diagnosis; establish a plan to confirm that diagnosis; establish a treatment plan; educate the patient to the plan; assure that the patient opts in and will be working with me.

The way in which we communicate will help me reach the final goal, and I will adjust to achieve that end. I don't really modify the other goals—work around, maybe, modify according to the exigencies of an insurer's requirements or a personal issue, possibly, vary the timing for a variety of reasons, sometimes—because they are the heart and soul of what I do.

While most people think the point of a consultation is to make a diagnosis, and establish a treatment plan, in other words, identify and fix the problem, for me consultation goes deeper than this. Figuring out the problem is not as hard as it might seem. The number of possible causes of a set of symptoms is usually finite; sometimes there are several to choose from, but mostly it boils down to an obvious half dozen or so possible diagnoses.

Occasionally a weird diagnosis appears—I have seen strange infections, poisonings, and cancer mimicking arthritis or autoimmune disease—but unusual diagnoses almost always follow careful observation and questioning; they do not serendipitously just pop into mind. A doctor can smell them out, if the examination is compulsively done and inconsistencies pursued.

As for tests, there generally aren't that many. A handful of blood tests, X-rays, CT scans, MRIs, and some organ function tests as well. The trick is not to do those that aren't truly necessary, to focus quickly on the real culprit, not to throw out wide nets in the hope that some unsuspected fish will be caught. In chronic illness evolution of symptoms over time and careful physical examination tell more about diagnosis and prognosis than do liters of blood or gigabyte X-ray files.

The new patient and I have different understandings of what this visit is about. In her mind she is here for a few blood tests, maybe an X-ray or two, a straightforward matter: "I have a problem. Test for and find the problem. Solve it." That's the way it was for most of the acute medical conditions she may have encountered before. That's what television doctors do. That's what surgeons do. Appendicitis? Ovarian cyst? Breast lump? When in doubt, cut it out. A chance to cut is a chance to cure. Fell skiing, did you? Broke your leg? A cast, a pin, a crutch, and mostly you are healed. Infection? Here's an antibiotic. Rash? Use this cream. Pregnancy?—well, we know about those. A bit dicey, sometimes, a bit more of the unknown. But for this, she likely thinks, give me a pill and make me well.

Chances are she has not yet met a doctor who says, "I can't make you fully well. I'm certain of the diagnosis, I know all the treatments, I've seen hundreds of patients like you. I can make you better but I am not going to make you well." Or worse, "You're at the beginning of an illness that will evolve. It hasn't declared itself yet. It may turn into this, it may turn into that, or it may go away." And, "I can offer treatments that will ease it a bit but not more, and I can offer treatments that will make you feel wonderful but you will hate the side-effects." This is what I will teach her. This lesson will not be taught in one day, and I will barely begin today.

When I put a name to the problem she thinks—sometimes says out loud—"Oh, thank heavens, he knows what is wrong." A name gives her dignity, and hope, especially if other doctors or family or friends have dismissed her as overreacting to flu or depression. With the first few pills I prescribe often she feels almost miraculously well again. Euphoria takes over. She thinks I am a genius. She thinks that she is cured.

This is not my lesson. She is elated but I am not, so I choose not to pull her under the waterline with me. Absent foreknowledge, she sees relief from pain and normality's return, while I see future drug side effects, damage to joints and internal organs, relapses, and disruptions of the life she hopes to lead. I need not share all this with her right now. Lessons can be absorbed slowly; they are best given when the mind is prepared.

Instead, these are the lessons I will later share with her: this illness is not going to go away; there will be times that you will be well but at other times you will be ill; your life now has boundaries and uncertainty that you cannot have foreseen. You can marry, have a family (maybe), work (maybe), travel, but from now on you will carry a burden that others may— but often will not—comprehend.

You will meet physicians who know less about this illness than you do. It's up to you to understand what is happening to your body. You must be in charge, must educate your family and friends—your doctors, if need be. After a few years a good attitude, and a good line to trump arrogant young physicians, is: "I've had this illness since before you entered medical school." Or (for those who have been around a while) to new interns, "…since before you were born." For the older or pompous doctor, "I've lived with this for X years and you have not. My experience is as important as yours."

She will learn these lessons over time, whether I teach them or not. I need not force their comprehension today. I'm not that good a teacher. Most patients new to chronic disease hear what I say but do not believe. The lessons root more deeply when experienced personally than when heard. I may say, "You must take this medicine to feel well." She may think (but rarely says), "I don't like what it does to me. I feel well, so I'll bet that the illness is gone." She will consult friends, perhaps other doctors, the Internet, self-help groups, and will tell me she has done so or will not. I assume she has. I assume that at some point she will quit taking the medicine. When she does, she may suffer a "flare"(a recurrence of symptoms) or she may not. She will experiment with nutrition, alternative medicines, prayer, and magical cures.

I may not know the details, but I know that my advice will at one point be rejected and that testing will go on. I may or may not tell her I expect this to happen. When it does, I do not contest. I shrug and think to myself, "She'll learn, she'll learn." Pain is a good teacher and it usually alerts before damage is done. My rules are negotiable except when I say they are not. If I believed the experiment truly dangerous I would vigorously forewarn.

I trust her to tell me what matters. She trusts me to advise. We negotiate—I don't dictate—the next set of plans. The painful lessons help establish trust. I expect the experiment. That I gave her freedom to try, that my response is bemusement and not anger, translate to this: you are an adult, in charge of your own life. I counsel. You decide. If you accept that my training and experience validate my advice, you will tell me what you need, I will tell you what I want you to do, and together we will decide. This illness is not just your problem. It is our problem. Together. We will go forward—as partners, you in the lead.

MDL

The Girl in the Pink Snowsuit

The subject of power and chronic illness is complex, and one I have thought about a great deal, because I feel powerless much of the time. Yet, at those times when I have felt the weakest, people often have judged me to be the exact opposite. Ironically, in my weakest passages, I have been judged to be controlling of the lives of others or acting in a manipulative manner. Such is the misunderstood presumption of the false power of illness. It is a phenomenon only those with a serious chronic condition can fully comprehend.

What do I mean by referring to it as a false form of power? Simply put, it happens when I become suddenly dysfunctional and can't do something I had promised previously I would do in good faith. This is also what I mean when I refer to the "inconvenience of chronic illness." When I am in fairly good shape, the seemingly smallest thing can change my status from stable to quite unwell. It could be a cold I have not paid enough attention to in its earliest stages, a particularly high pollen count in allergy season, too many sleepless nights, or even inhaled smoke from a brush fire more than two hillsides or three towns away. Over the years I have learned to gauge how much I take on and under what terms and conditions, yet, there are still times when I am unable to do something I pledged I would do for someone else. From the moment I "crash" I know explanations will be fairly pointless.

When I was younger I spent a lot of energy needlessly attempting to explain my sudden lapses in letters, phone calls and, in the last few years, emails in my attempts to communicate what the healthy simply can't really grasp. It has taken many years to calculate that at these times, virtually any form of explanation puts me in a no-win situation, and bound to be misinterpreted.

In my perhaps overly zealous resolution never to succumb to the notion that I am "illness" more than I am "Alida", I give the impression of being an unstoppable force. However, when the illness manifests itself, it results in a flat-out physical, mental and emotional shutdown. Others can't understand that unless they too have experienced illness themselves, or have carefully observed what really happens in these times, and have stood by me, and with me, during such episodes. Only a few can do that.

The fact that I am not following through on a promise, not delivering on a request, not reading or returning emails, not communicating fully on the telephone may seem as though I need to be in control of a situation. In reality, I am not controlling anything or anyone; I can't even control my body's unruly systemic outbursts. At times, my silence has been interpreted as rejection, or hostility, or anger. What it is, of course, is the result of total exhaustion. An exhaustion or feeling of fatigue that is so severe it can render me useless to myself as well as to others.

After all these years I still find it hard to accept that some friends just "don't get it" and they never will. They think it's like the flu, or a bad muscle strain; it will go away. So, why can't I hurry up and recover? —So that their lives and work not be inconvenienced? It can't be helped. Power is a complicated issue with human beings even if everyone is on a level playing field with equal status and the rules of the game fully understood by all.

I came to the hospital one day to talk to Michael about some changes and additions we were thinking about making to the manuscript for this book. It was a particularly cold day and a busy one at the hospital. Despite many expensive renovations and improvements, the elevator system remains inadequate to serve the needs of two large populations—patients and their families and friends, and the medical staff and administrators.When I feel sturdy, to avoid the crowded elevator I walk the six-plus flights up to Michael's office. I was not feeling all that sturdy on this particular day. I endured the usually interminable wait for an elevator to come, and one going in the correct direction. Everyone was jammed into it, as always. A girl and her mother got on with me, and I could see the little girl had badly crippled, or perhaps, deformed, hands.

She was wearing a pink snowsuit. She was a beautiful little girl. Then, I noticed she did not walk well, so I made an assumption her feet and/or her legs might be similarly afflicted. I smiled at her, but she was too busy holding on to her mother, to the best of her ability.

Just as the door was about to close, a tall, thin and elegant doctor got on the elevator. He clearly was in a dark mood. I read doctors' faces well; I could tell instantly that he was not having a good day.

The little girl got squeezed between her mother and the doctor. Somehow, in her attempt not to topple over, she stepped on his expensive shoes. I would say they were probably Italian shoes and cost more than her entire snowsuit. The little girl moved away quickly; the mother apologized.

The doctor said angrily, "Can't you keep her to the other side of you? She stepped on my shoes." I thought it interesting that he said the word "shoes." I would have said, "excuse me but you've stepped on my toes,"or "ouch, you've crunched my feet." However, I wouldn't have said a word, even if I had been wearing solid gold slippers, to this little girl, already a full-fledged member in the world of the forever limited. The mother apologized far too profusely it seemed to me. The doctor folded his arms. Power had asserted itself into the exchange.

He looked down and glared at the little girl. I stared at him with burning contempt, but he did not notice me, or sense my anger. He was too involved looking at his precious shoes to assess the damage, if any.

The door opened on another floor. More people shoved their way into an almost filled-to-capacity elevator car. As it would happen, the little girl, unsteady and unsure, got shoved along with the new passengers, and once again, she landed on the doctor's shoes. He lost it. There is no elegant or literary phrase to dress up what he did or said. I leaned down and gently touched the sleeve of the girl's snowsuit. "This is a beautiful pink snowsuit. I'll bet it is new. Did you get it for Christmas?" She looked in my eyes; there were tears in hers. She nodded yes to me. I said, "You must be a very good girl to have received such a wonderful snowsuit."

I looked away from her, because I did not want her to see the tears in my own eyes, the tears of rage—my own powerless rage.

I got off at Michael's floor, and went into his office. And, then—I lost it.

Some day in the future, a woman in her fifties, (hopefully) will arrive in a kindly doctor's office for an examination or a consultation for her ongoing health problems. But, that doctor will not know or have any ability to see that somewhere buried inside that woman will be a tiny girl, in a pink snowsuit, in a crowded elevator, who once many decades earlier offended a tall and powerful doctor.

There is no way that any doctor can know when he first sees a patient what scars she hides, not only from her illness, but from the past abuses of medical power. Power between a doctor and a patient is never distributed equally. It is always present as a potentially insurmountable obstacle to a sick person's recovery and return to the realm of self-esteem and identity, if not full health.

Whatever was wrong with that doctor's life that day is both unimportant and irrelevant to me. Perhaps he had just experienced the death of a patient he cared about deeply. Perhaps he had just been in a particularly unpleasant meeting with a colleague. Perhaps he had called home and had a serious fight with a wife, a companion, a lover. No matter. The damage was done—maybe irreparable damage—not to his shoes, but to the little girl.

The doctor had the power to choose which would be more important to him in that instant. He also had the power to keep his mouth shut, but chose instead his expensive shoes.

AB

One Up, One Down

Strange to say, I had always thought that the patient-doctor dialogue begins the moment I walk through the examining room door to meet with a patient. I was wrong, of course. I had not thought the matter through. I only enter the story at the second act. How could I have been in this business for so many years and not known that which is so obviously true?

The dialogue between a patient and doctor begins long before I first hear the patient's name. Somewhere out there, in a world I do not know, a person feels ill or is told of an abnormal blood test, or in some other way senses a change. This moment, in her mind but not yet manifest by any deed, opens a door. That door opens a passage out from her comfortable, self-contained world, a passage that, in turn, leads into my world. By crossing this threshold, she opens her up-to-now private existence to a total stranger.

Although she may still consider this a business transaction—the car makes a noise, she finds someone who can fix it; a wedding needs planning, one can purchase the services of someone who does this for a living—she may intuit, and I certainly know, that this transaction encompasses much more. There is a driving force, a state of constant unwellness that will most likely assume an unwanted control of her life. The quantity and quality of that force will dictate my response. A car can be junked; a body cannot. A wedding can be re-sited or rescheduled or redesigned. A body that goes wrong does so in a time and place that we do not choose and at a rate that is only barely subject to personal will.

Somewhere a person, whose name and personality remain unknown to me, talks to a relative or friend, or to her personal doctor, or she seeks out some other information source, and she learns my name. She may hunt for an explanation of her symptoms on the Internet. She may leaf through brochures or advertisements or even the telephone book. Then she decides to make a call.

Her side of the dialogue has begun. (At the moment it is only a monologue). Her telephone call will be necessarily supplicative. Of necessity she will have chosen to surrender at least a bit of control over her person and her dignity. After all, she certainly knows that she will have to admit imperfection and must assume that she will be asked to disclose many very private things to a person she has not met.

This circumstance is not unique. People see doctors all the time. But I doubt they ever know exactly what to expect, at least if they have any inkling that this is the beginning of chronic disease, and that this relationship may last a very long time.

She picks up a phone and makes the call. I imagine this moment to be like a teenager calling for a first date, picking up the telephone and putting it down, and picking it up perhaps several more times. Dialing halfway, then stopping. Putting it off and hoping the need to make the call will disappear. But I never talk to patients about this time.

The telephone rings in my office. Someone in my office answers. Throughout my professional life I have been fortunate to have superb people working with me. They are, I believe, warm and sympathetic and helpful, but, of course, I do not know how warm and friendly my assistants sound to the caller on the other end.

The next part of the conversation is all business. I imagine it can be potentially upsetting given its impersonal nature: what insurance I do or do not accept, what are the co-pays, am I the right person to see, what appointments are available, how much time will the appointment take, what will I do, straightforward stuff but off-putting if the answers are not those desired.

An appointment is made. The day arrives; other indignities follow. First there is traffic. Since I work in a large city, in a neighborhood not easily accessible by public transportation, I know that the trek in for a consultation can be terrifying for many suburbanites and for people from small rural towns. Parking is in short supply and expensive. My hospital is part of an imposing medical complex that covers more than six city blocks, both sides of the street. To add to the confusion, the main entrance is off a side street, on which there has been construction for many years (different projects, no intervals between), with directional signs hidden or taken down: confusing, easy to get lost.

The hospital lobby is pleasant but not palatial. Security guards man the front door. They are not threatening. They are more like doormen, but they are reminders that one lives in a post 9-11 world. Like essentially everyone in our hospital, the lady at the reception/information desk, whom I have known for years, is friendly and helpful. Still, one cannot hide the fact that the lobby is often crowded with people in wheelchairs and children with congenital deformities waiting for medical transport vans to take them home. The overall scene is not reassuring to a first-time visitor. The elevators to my office floor are slow and crowded. New ones are being built: another construction project that, as I write, has taken more than a year.

Due to hospital bureaucracy a new patient does not report directly to my office but instead is sent to a moderately large reception area. A receptionist, always pleasant but sometimes new and confused, asks the patient to fill out more forms, then asks her to sit among other patients, many of whom are visibly very ill and obviously impaired: more frightening reminders to the prospective patient.

Once the receptionist notifies my office that the patient has arrived, a nurse escorts her to an examining room. (I no longer have the luxury of interviewing her in my office first.) She is weighed in a public area (clothed, fortunately, but people dislike disclosing their weights) and measured and assessed for blood pressure, pulse, and temperature. The nurses are cheerful and gregarious. The examining rooms themselves are bare and unimaginative, but not threatening, no awful surgical instruments on display.

At my request—other doctors do it differently—the nurses do not ask the patient to undress. I prefer that my first sight of the patient be as she wishes to be seen. To be sure, I will examine her undressed in a short while, but not now. (The indignity of undressing goes both ways: I will have to keep a straight face when I see the hidden and sometimes embarrassing tattoos, the navel rings or, God help me, the nipple rings!)

At this point the monologue becomes dialogue—except, I now understand that the starting line for the patient began long before I entered the examining room. I had not thought this process through. I had not considered how the run-up to the appointment effectively turns our relationship into a me-up, you-down contact.

Then we meet: I am in white coat uniform, she in street clothing. She has come to my place, not the other way around. She called for permission to come. I have initials after my name, credentials displayed on the door and on the wall. I am male, she (usually) female. I am generally older than she, sometimes her parents' (or grandparents'!) age. When we first meet she is sitting but I stand. There is no equality here. Even were the point of the visit to be different, she is in every sense the supplicant and I the grantor.

This therefore cannot be a dialogue of equals. She understands or intuits that she has lost control of her body to illness—that is, after all why she is here—and that she must now surrender at least a part of her body to me.

Me up, she down—that is what I believe she sees. For most of the time, an accurate depiction of how we relate. It is not very likely, I think, that she spends much time considering how she (or her illness) control me. For practical purposes, I am always on call. If she cannot plan her day, neither can I. A sudden fever, shortness of breath, a seizure, certain types of pain get an instant response, day or night, three hundred and sixty-five days a year. I don't feel much more in control than does she. My days are dictated by events not under my control.

That's not such a big deal (except, I assume, to my family). I accepted that when I entered this profession. The real point is that she can act and get me to respond at any time—a vulnerability on my part of which I am very aware. Except: her exercising this control is almost never willed. It occurs in a moment of fright, sometimes justified, sometimes not; but it is never planned.

I do not and cannot assume that she ever sees an emergency call as a me-up, you-down situation. But in the totality of my broken nights and weekends, she has far more control than she believes. If we are both lucky, what I will be able to do is hand back knowledge and control to her. The ideal outcome of this encounter will be that she will handle her errant organs and physiology by herself, that she will exit my world, that she will shut the connecting door, and return to her own self-contained world.

We may not be so lucky. The disease may settle in. If we stay together, she will begin to understand over the next several visits my approach and my limits; I will better understand her strengths and possibilities. It is not likely that our dialogue will ever approach a conversation of equals, because the social structure of our encounter does not permit it to go this way.

Chances are that she will always call me Doctor—I never ask patients to, but they almost always do—a verbal signal that I am in charge, a magical verbal symbol imputing omniscience, or at least ability to provide an answer, to me. Unless she is a child or a personal friend I do not call her by her first name, and the formality establishes a (to me unnecessary, but a sociologist may disagree) distance in our relationship. Although in times of her good health the balance scale of our relationship will move toward the horizontal, in the back of my mind I am always aware, as I think she is, that if things worsen I will assume control of her body and, to some extent, her mind.

We will talk to one another, we will negotiate about the edges, but she will probably always feel that I hold the upper hand. I cannot change this relationship nor can she, except by her choosing not to return to me. We can pretend that there is equality. I can hope that I will be able to keep arrogance at bay, that I will emphasize her dignity, that I will hear her out, and that I will always ask her assent for what I am about to do. I can hope for this and that she will call me to task if I fail.

MDL

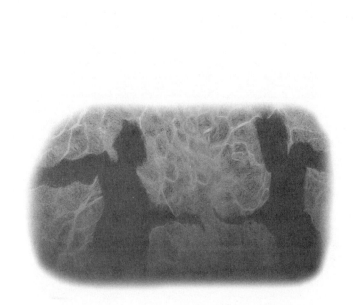

3
An Unstable Life

A Hawk in Winter

Alida is traveling afar. We have exchanged a few email messages, and the messages cause me concern. Staring out my window on a quiet Saturday afternoon, I reflect about how moods and lives change in an instant. Predictions are accurate or they fail. Plans are made and then set aside. Chronic illness remits and flares again. Interruptions are the only constant.

So it is with patients and with their doctors. They see and confront the unexpected—but from different sides. When they work together, they attack the intrusion from two flanks at once. Together they form a team that is stronger than either would be alone.

It is a quiet Saturday afternoon, two days before Christmas, in upstate New York. The day is unseasonably warm. The temperature outside is fifty-three degrees. The sky is blue and the sun is bright. A heavy rain had fallen most of the previous night. At my desk, in front of my computer, I glance out a floor-to-ceiling window facing north. The grass on the lawn is a healthy green, the color of a late summer day. Mountain laurel bushes arranged close in, spruce and cedar trees form a windbreak further out, everything verdant, filling the view. Although the calendar says late December, winter seems months away.

Lazily I swivel my chair toward the opposite side and gaze out the western windows set high in the wall. My chair being low, I can look up and see the leafless branches and tree trunks of a deciduous forest: a winter scene, at least in fantasy, skeletons of oaks and maples and tulip trees, taller than the conifers, no spruce on this side. The radio, background to my work, plays Christmas music non-stop. I am not in a Christmas mood so I spin the dial (it is an old radio). "Saturday Afternoon at the Opera" is playing *Don Carlo*. The story is that of the Inquisition—autos-da-fé and all—but the music is lovely and fits my mood; I prefer the opera to the carols, and so I select this station. Staring through the black tracery of the branches, I imagine snow covering the low-lying green flora behind me, a dream winter, correct according to the calendar, but giving lie to the reality outside.

The sky is without wind; the branches are still—a peaceful hibernal scene. Peaceful, that is, until, from the right, first a shadow, moving rapidly on a graceful, curvilinear path, becomes a large round object with an indistinct edge, then halts, snaps into focus, softly shakes itself, stretches and folds its wings, turns its head to the right then the left, and shows itself as a large red-tailed hawk, dominant, silent, staring down from a high branch of a young oak. His arrival takes but a few seconds, a short time, indeed, but an event of an instant can change the mood of the day.

I know this hawk. He visits our little forest often. He is impressive, and deadly still, save for the slow rotation and occasional tilt of the broad head and great hooked beak. I am now alert, anticipating: at a particular moment his head will fix for a few seconds at an angle, then noiselessly and with barely a hint of body motion he will plunge with lightning speed at an angle nearly perpendicular to the earth. There will be a brief moment of violence, scattered leaves, some fur in the air but little blood, and a sudden, anguished squeak from his prey. In the next few seconds, often without even stopping, he will fly off at a thirty to forty-five degree angle to the ground, dangling a motionless mouse or squirrel or other creature in his claws. Reality trumps the dream. It tends to do that. Especially in winter.

So too with chronic illness. It does not go away. In chronic illness dreams are commonplace. Sudden violent interruptions occur. There is a point at which every patient imagines herself free of illness, fully vital, no swollen joints, no lost hair, no marks of drug effects, physically vibrant; in fact, well. Every doctor, at some time, shares that dream. Yet, from my side, I know—or fear—that the bad times will come again.

Sometimes they grow slowly, a little perturbance of normality, a nothing, a minor blip in well-being, that gets better; then another perturbance, perhaps larger a few days or weeks later; and another, until either the doctor or the patient begins to understand that this remission is over and the dream has fled. More often it is like the hawk: a shadow becomes a visible threat, then, in a brief instant, incalculable violence occurs.

The disease is back. The mood is broken, the fantasy dissolved. A cry of despair announces the change.

My first job is clear: to regain control. I have no access to the patient's point of view. I can only surmise what she must feel. Despair has got be present, or anxiety at least. My other job is to conquer the despair, to maintain optimism, to keep the patient with me, to keep her on the same team, fighting together, to push the illness back underground again—whether or not I believe that it can be done.

You can track the mood changes in the email exchanges. Here are the words of a young professional woman, mid-twenties, seriously ill a few years ago, now feeling well, anxious to move to the next phase (there is a young man in her life right now) and anxious to stop her medications with unpleasant side effects, a possibility we had discussed if her blood tests looked good. Here is her dream. The translation of this exchange is: I do not want to believe that I am ill any more.

Patient, August 21

Hello, did you happen to get my blood test results back?
Have a great week!

ML, August 21

You are in good shape. Want to negotiate?

Patient, August 21

I'm ALWAYSSSSS ready to negotiate!!!!! What do you think?????
:)

ML, August 21

Okay, so long as you understand that you have about a one in three chance of having recurrence of disease and are willing to take that chance.

Patient, August 21

Yes, I understand…I'm a little nervous but if I am the ONE [who does not have recurrence]…I'll be the happiest person in the world, that's why for me it's worth taking a chance!

I am really excited!!!!!!! Xooxoxoxox

Thank soooooooooo much…I'll keep you posted.

I am happy for her but I can't really share her joy. I see the silent, watching hawk; she does not. She is doing well now, but I fear that at some time in the future the disease will come back. I don't know when. It might not. So for the moment I don't disabuse her. Let her live her life and be joyful. Let the dream remain.

But there is little magic in this world, and even writing this book is no amulet to ward off bad times. This book was conceived at a time when Alida was well, a time that could not be sustained in the long term. Follow her emails, then, as they lead to my ruminations.

August 6
Believe it or not, I've not touched a drop of respiratory meds here. The air here is sweet and clean.

September 11
I'm doing quite fine, really…

September 25
Have had some really nasty fevers the last two nights…can Cytoxan do that? Do feel considerably better today, but weakened by the fevers.

December 4
Hi there. It seems as if the Cytoxan @ two a day just isn't holding this back totally. Some "thinning" on the elbows which is beginning to look not so promising and breathing stuff, and rip-roaring-bone-crunching joint pain which comes and goes but shoots through me fairly seriously…are we back for a sniff of the needle routine [giving the medication intravenously], or do you want to hold for now?????????

December 5
Magic wand time.

December 22
Am still having something going on. And I feel frankly, quite

wretched and disgusted with the whole nonsense of this thing. It's in charge. I respect it for that, it is inventive, clever, devious and tough, and when I stand back from it…it impresses me. But I am in it, not standing back from it. I had another moderate fever spike last night.102, most of the night, crested to 103 about 3 a.m. then down again…back to normal at about 6 a.m. Shooting pains through joints remain. Elbows now active.

I am going to gut this out…NO MORE DRUGS…I can't…I just can't. The drugs cause a meta-disease of their own, as you know. I am ready to just play this out and see what happens. I am weary of this, Mike, it's a game, and I am walking away from the betting table right now.

I'm pretty much down to the…let's just let it have its own way…I've been struggling now with this for 3 years without one break.

There comes a time, when the fatigue sets in with even the most valiant warrior. I need to put down my sword and let it be.

NO, I am not playing the doctor, I am playing Alida, and this is what I can handle right now. What more can I do?

I feel just as lousy w/ drugs as I feel when I am sick. And, we're not exactly preserving me for some fantastic life now, let's be frank, for heaven's sake…we don't need to go into the high red alert we did when I was 28!

This is the bad time. It is impossible to sustain the dream right now. Yet beneath the discouragement, there is a push-pull: who is in control, the disease or the person? The doctor or the patient? Likely all four are in combat.

Reinforcing the person is an important part of my job. Her life is not threatened at this point. I know that I can relax a bit, reduce the dose of the toxic medication by putting her on one less toxic, maybe nature will heal her a little bit. She thinks so too, and she knows the disease better than I do; she has lived with it longer than I have. At a distance of 3,000 miles I watch for danger signals that would cause me to become imperious and to assert control. I haven't seen those signals yet, but I do worry that I am wrong.

Another patient emails me almost daily, and sometimes many times a day. For more than two years I have not been able to help her in her current crisis. When she tries to eat she vomits or has she has unbearable abdominal pain. We have done many tests, consulted surgeons and several gastroenterologists, to no avail. She tells me and tells me again, in person and by email, that she will never get well.

I am a born optimist. I continue to believe that the right clue, the right test, the right consultant—one of us will solve this thing and return (a degree of) normality to her. The leitmotif of this email is insuppressible doom, but moments of hope shine through. It is these moments that make me believe that I can keep her on my side, that we can partner together, and together we can overcome.

November 6
I had a severe choking/coughing episode today after drinking broth. Anyway, the speech therapist was within earshot and she came over. She told me to chin tuck to swallow. I laughed and said I wasn't 90 and demented yet…I am close[r] to demented [than to] 90.

December 5
One good thing about the IV [cortisone she had just received], no joint pain :)

December 6
I am running an on and off 101 temp today. Coughing up yellow junk. I have to be better by tomorrow due to work.

December 8
Looking like Rudolph [the red-nosed reindeer].

December 15
Attempted to eat earlier today. Ate and ate and then vomited and vomited. Quite a bit of blood and continuing to cough up blood.

Sorry…but I don't care.

Have a nice holiday and weekend.

December 20
Severe pain all night.

I have to finish up my holiday shopping today, asking for a couple of days pain-free….

January 4
In hindsight…I wish I didn't [see another consultant] and I would have died eventually. Then there would be no more pain, disappointment, frustration and mystery for everyone involved. I think one could learn more with autopsy.

January 5
Sorry about the tone of my last email. You are the only reason I go to my appointments. I would feel like I was disappointing you if I didn't go. It has nothing to do with feeling hopeful.

The hawk did not dive down. He stayed a while then flew away to sate his hunger in other woods. The sun has gone down early. In winter, it always does. Elizabeth and Don Carlo escape the Inquisition in glorious ascending chords as the opera draws to a close. The temperature will be in the 30's tomorrow. Dream and reality will merge.

Alfred Lord Tennyson wrote about this contradiction that is no contradiction, about how dreams and anguish coincide:

So runs my dream; but what am I?
An infant crying in the night;
An infant crying for the light,
And with no language but a cry.

Today there shall be no anguished cry from a small furry creature on the ground. The disease flare-ups of my email correspondents will abate. The young optimist will remain off medications; the young man in her life will become her fiance.

The dream is not destroyed. It has been restrained for a little bit. Tennyson's cry has the power to become a voice with a language, to assert control. The hawk was here but has gone. Winter will end. The flare will be over. Chronic illness will be beaten back and forced underground. This time. Until the next time. Until we finally and permanently win this war. Human resilience and spirit remain.

MDL

The Bitter Pill

We are sitting in a chic gourmet café and cheese shop in the Los Feliz district of Los Angeles, California, two attractive women of a certain age. She has blonde hair, smartly cut, just above her shoulders, and I'm a reddish blonde, my hair is very short, closely cropped to my head. We are both interestingly dressed, with close attention paid to minute details in our choice of earrings and accessories.

We have similar styles—artistic, a bit of elegant bohemian, not professional or matronly. She has a fair complexion, as do I. She is dressed in shades of aquamarine. Her sweater and scarf layered, her eyes of liquid intensity. I am dressed in shades of persimmon and burnt sienna. I wear two layers of sweaters and two scarves, one silk, the other one, cashmere. It is the cashmere one that I have around my throat, although it is a warm day.

We appear to be strong and confident women, and yet, also somehow oddly fragile. We are engaged in a quiet, almost secretive, conversation. Our heads come together over a shared cheese platter and two glasses of red wine.

"Do you remember the first time? How old were you?" I ask her.

"I remember it vividly, of course, who can forget that sort of thing? I was seventeen. How about you?"

"Me? Are you kidding? I was twelve."

"What do you remember the most about that first time?"

"How bitter it was. How about you?" I sip my wine as I await her answer.

"I remember saying to myself 'this is a tiny defeat.' What I thought is that there would be more, larger ones, bigger defeats." She sighs as she reaches for a bunch of grapes on the cheese platter.

"Yes, that's just it, isn't it? First the tiny defeat, and then, the larger ones, and then…"

We both knowingly study each other and say in unison,

"The little deaths…."

I lost much of my hair to the chemotherapy. When it began to grow back, I decided to keep it very short, just in case. My good friend, Erika has chronic and at times, debilitating asthma. As we were having this conversation, we realized the younger women sitting next to us were listening in rapt attention. Understandably, they thought we were talking about our first sexual experiences. That's when I said to Erika, "We are in Los Angeles. Call script rewrite. Let's do this scene differently. No. Wait! Let's do our whole damn lives differently. I want a new screenplay, please. Right now!" We laughed and laughed, as we do when we are together, especially when one of us, or both of us, is particularly plagued by our chronic problems.

This particular afternoon, I was the weaker one, although neither of us had been terribly well. There had been a brush fire more than a week before, a few hillsides away from where we were having our lunch. Inevitably I sustained smoke inhalation, which angered an already fragile respiratory system.

Despite the number of days that had elapsed since the fire, I was still almost voiceless and in considerable pain. The lining of my lungs was inflamed and felt as if it too were on fire. We were whispering because I could not speak above that level, and because Erika's oxygen supply wasn't superb that day either. Despite how lousy we felt, (exhausted, depressed, wheezing) we had both spent an inordinate amount of time choosing our clothing, applying make-up, and fixing our hair. We tend to do that, especially when we're worn down by disease but determined to stay in the battle and somehow manage to stay upright. Erika jokingly refers to this behavior as our "Pretty Girls Rule!" moments.

Although we have been friends for a long time, we have known each other only as chronically ill adult women. We were not younger women or girls together, although we were both ill as teenagers. She found out about my illness during our first meeting, before the friendship evolved. I had admired her work for years, and finally went to a gallery where she was represented. They contacted her and we met. I purchased a small watercolor of hers that particularly appealed to me. I still love it. It goes where I go; it's probably earned the right to have a passport of its own. I bought the painting for myself on what was then a significant birthday, a milestone I had not expected I would reach. The painting was my small reward. Uncharacteristically, I told her why that birthday mattered to me, although she was a total stranger. She said she understood such things. After that first encounter, we met again briefly for lunch; it was then she told me about her life-long battle with asthma.

To anyone observing us in the café that afternoon, we looked like the kind of artistic women who just might be talking about their first love affairs, or current ones, or about-to-be-past ones. The young women were right to eavesdrop. They were just way off about the topic. We had been talking about the fact that, despite fatigue and pain, I was trying to continue to write this book. I was annoyed because I had to interrupt my work so often to take naps as well as to use a variety of "lung toys" to ease my breathing.

We then turned to discuss our relationships with a most familiar companion, the drug prednisone. I wanted to write about the way it felt the first time I had taken it. I wondered about her first time. Far from telling stories about lost virginity, we were telling a far more intimate and revealing secret; we were talking about what has come to dictate, or control, at least part of our lives: the use of steroids in the treatment of chronic autoimmune illness.

Erika is just a little older than I am in calendar years, but in *katun* measurement, we have been at this about the same amount of time. (She takes more prednisone than I do at this point, and the side effects are often dreadful for her. I do not take much or any of it now, because I must take more toxic drugs, with different side effects.) Even after the passage of all the years, she said each time she swallows the pill it feels like "a tiny defeat." I knew what she meant. She needs the drug in order to survive; yet, even the smallest dose is part of her daily realization she will never be completely without the illness, or without prednisone.

When I swallowed my first batch of steroid pills, I recall vividly how bitter they tasted. "What a bitter pill," I thought, "These pills have a bad taste." The girl I was then did not understand that eventually this "bitter pill" would stand as a metaphor for my life. Almost a full *katun* would expire before I understood I was never going to be well, although I would experience periods of health and renewed strength. I was almost thirty before I finally accepted, without any question, that my disease would never go away. It would change its performance patterns, sometimes at alarming speeds, but it would never go away.

I should have understood this earlier when I was in my twenties and living in the Midwest. I was a young woman and Michael Lockshin was as yet a person unknown to me. He was just then beginning his career as a chronic disease specialist in autoimmune phenomena. Michael was launching what would become a distinguished and brilliant career. I meanwhile was already more than a decade into my own career of managing a personal life with what he was choosing to spend his professional life exploring and attempting to outsmart. He was already working on my behalf. Although at that time there was no reason to understand, or contemplate, a world where we would someday work together as fellow warriors, let alone collaborators on a book.

In a large university teaching hospital in the Midwest, I encountered the only physician I can never ever forgive. He was exceedingly arrogant, too handsome, fairly young and on the quest for diagnosis, whatever the cost or risk to me. My disease was a puzzle and had been since my early years. There was the suspicious occurrence of rheumatic fever at age six that led some rheumatologists down one path or a series of them, and others, judging it irrelevant, not down any. The absolute belief that it was JRA (juvenile rheumatoid arthritis) had been abandoned because after years of throbbing and swollen joints, which were disfigured during the flares, I had absolutely no joint damage. In the middle of an otherwise peaceful period, in the somewhat boring, but also exceedingly cozy, Midwest, I awoke one night with alarm. My entire body was swollen and throbbing. I was also experiencing extreme chest pain. The ambulance took me to the university hospital, where I was put into intensive care.

After days of steroid dripping into me via an IV, the symptoms were gone, but the blood tests were questionable. I had pulled a failing grade on a test I had not yet heard about, until that moment. It was called an ANA, and the results were of great interest to the doctor and what appeared to me to be an army of residents, interns and casual observers, all in white coats, all in charge. Not one of them expressed their awareness that a very frightened young woman was inside the system that they had created around the person.

The system was the kind of medicine then practiced in a large teaching hospital where the goal was virtually always centered on diagnosis. I must have given my life's story to at least two dozen medical students within three days, to residents, as well as to senior doctors and specialists. After all, it was a research and teaching hospital connected to a university. I did not understand I could decline to speak further to them. I did not understand I could say I was too tired, or too sick or in too much pain. I just kept going over it again and again. I thought I had been enrolled in an ongoing graduate seminar and, of course, I wanted to be the smartest girl in the discussion. I wanted to be the "best girl" and I wanted them to like me.

Finally, a package with the results of lab work and a slide of a biopsy of a strange thing on my elbow was shipped to a very important doctor in New York. At that point in my life, New York was only the place of immature dreams. These fantasies were romantic and sentimental—I thought of New York as it was depicted in Hollywood movies. *Breakfast at Tiffany's, A Love Affair to Remember,* that sort of thing. I am not proud of this confession, but there it is. I grew up in California. In my mind, New York was the place of sheer romance, not medical science at the cutting edge of discovery. At that time, there was no Fed-ex, Express Mail, fax, or the Internet, or any of these timesaving tools we have come to rely on. It took a few days to get the results. The brash, and always impatient, young doctor in charge of me stormed into my room.

"Well, we finally have the results," he announced brusquely.

"Good or bad?" I asked with a feeling of tremendous foreboding.

"Depends, on what you want. You do not have SLE." I did not know what that meant. He had not bothered to tell me what they were looking for, and so I had to ask him. He couldn't understand I did not know what he meant by SLE. His usual impatience peaked further; he was through with me. He couldn't find out what was going on with me. I was fired. The vast amount of steroid had gotten rid of whatever it was. He was going to give me an Rx to take lots more of it. He was already writing up the discharge papers for me to leave. Diagnosis was his goal. I had failed his only relevant test.

"What is that?"

"Lupus. You don't have lupus."

"That's good," I said. I did know what lupus was. I more or less knew, it had been mentioned in passing a few times, because of the childhood facial rashes and the frequent fevers.

"Good?"

"Yes, I mean that's good that I don't have lupus. Lupus is awful, isn't it?"

He was out the door; I saw his back heading to the exit of the cubicle where I had been placed in a step-down unit to intensive care. Barely turning around, I could only see his profile as he barked at me, "Well, at least if it were SLE, I would have my diagnosis."

I never saw him again, but kept swallowing the pills I had remembered from childhood. It was again the time of the bitter pills. I took them all, refilled them, again and again. I kept taking them until I was as manic as a monkey and had a face the size of a full Halloween moon in a comic book.

One day a casual friend told me she saw a Chinese herbalist for a fairly serious ongoing problem with colitis. I went to a pretty funky part of town and met an ancient Chinese woman. She looked at the pills, and threw them into the wastebasket with silent disgust and disdain.

Armed with vast amounts of tea sachets filled with God-knows-what, I left her office. I also had a variety of capsules filled with things she had ground and smashed while I was there. During the time I was with her, she talked to me softly. I asked no questions. I had nothing to say, all I knew for sure was that I was not going to take the Bitter Pill again. Nor did I intend to ever risk again meeting a doctor who would tell me a diagnosis was his ultimate victory.

I liked the Chinese herbalist. I got better, for a time. Mostly, I wasn't sad. I wasn't bloated. I was thin again. I wasn't anxious. I wasn't in pain. I was probably in a spontaneous remission. I believe she had knowledge gleaned from her ancient culture, not her age, (she was probably in her 70s!). She had wisdom Western medicine had not yet chosen to acknowledge, let alone accept. She probably had given me something that caused my prednisone withdrawal to be gentle, or at least tolerable.

It was the woman herself that I recall, however; she had a tender manner and a soothing voice. She took my pulses several times a visit. During the course of many appointments, she would put her fingers on certain places and apply strong pressure. Now, of course, I know she was practicing a form of acupressure, or some other form of Asian treatment. As I look back on my experiences with her, I believe her procedures were far less primitive than the ones that I had experienced in the university hospital.

There were enough warning signs during the years leading up to the encounter with Dr. Diagnosis for me to have understood, that my disease, although without a name at that point, was permanent. I was unwilling to face it; I was unwilling to believe medical science was not going to find the right drug. I cared so much about the right drug and so little about the right name for the disease. Mostly, I continued right through this period utterly convinced I was at the center of the problem. It had to be about me. I had caused it. Somehow, I had made these events happen. I just couldn't connect the dots to get the full picture of what I was doing wrong.

My mother was positive it was her fault. Between blaming myself, and comforting my mother, my energy was drained. I just wanted new and better drugs, and ones that really worked, not an intellectual journey of discovery. (My mother had never recovered from the loss of her first born, a son, who had died after a sudden and strange episode of high fevers. Finally, when I was in my 40's, a doctor friend looked at the charts and medical reports she had kept all those years, and concluded he had died most certainly of measles meningitis. That diagnosis was not a victory; it came far too late to improve her mental health.)

When I moved to Berkeley, California my attitude changed dramatically. My illness began to feel more like an adventure of discovery. I was at one of the university's major research institutes, where I was involved in running national opinion and attitude surveys. My circle of close friends and colleagues were other research scholars, academics, scientists as well as a plentiful supply of doctors.

It was also the dawn of the early collaboration between traditional medicine and the sorts of medicine that I had experienced with the loving Chinese herbal doctor. Words not previously spoken together were beginning to be placed under a new rubric: the body-mind connection. Berkeley, by then much quieter politically, was still, however, the kind of place open to collaborations and new definitions of all sorts. Almost everybody in my social circle had either seen, or was about to see, or knew someone being seen, by a particular individual. A professor and physician, who was also a psychiatrist, this man was considered the Bay Area's leading proponent of the body-mind connection.

I made an appointment with him and saw him at least three times a week, for some months. I rather more than adored him. Of course, he was primarily a shrink, and not a hands-on physician, which was totally new for me. He didn't perform nasty tests or tell me anything was my fault or tell me to take steroids. He talked at length about the connections the mind can make to help the body heal. At this point in my life, I have no objective point of view of whether or not he was absolutely brilliant or an overly zealous new age advocate. It does not matter. There was no question that he was extraordinarily smart, and was the first doctor with whom I came into contact who worked hard to make me understand that none of it, whether the disease had a name or not, was my fault.

Unlike the millions of his successors in the field of alternative medicine, he never claimed that the sick person caused her own problems. He never attributed my disease to unhappiness or suggested I was eating myself alive because something was "eating me." He also refused to endorse the notion that someone as sick as I could manage without traditional medical treatment.

He saw what he did as an addition or a complement to whatever the rheumatologists were doing, or in the process of deciding what they might do. However, he taught me the power of fasting and reducing the amount of meat in my diet, and these practices gave me added energy. As a bonus side benefit, he helped me take control of a potentially "lethal" professional interpersonal relationship. He got me to define the terms of that discourse, because he made me talk it through, but not the way ordinary shrinks do. He helped me come to an understanding of what I had to do in the way people of great wisdom help you talk about the truth, when it is buried too deeply for you to want to uncover it. I have no opinion about him as a medical doctor. In retrospect, I realize he was a guru to me, although that is a term I abhor. Let's put it this way—our bond was as close to the guru/student experience as I will encounter in my lifetime.

Ironically, he is the person who, probably unwittingly, led me to the new road, that I would, in time, walk down for the rest of my life. He nudged me toward the crossroads of two roads marked "Reality" and "Denial." One day I was sitting in his consulting room in the "Berkeley flats" discussing a vegetable juice regime I was about to embark on, when he stopped me mid-sentence. He got up, and walked toward the chair I was sitting in, but I wasn't alarmed. Clearly not a Freudian, he embraced or touched his patients from time to time. I thought he was probably coming over to take my hand to reduce my anxieties. He, did, in fact, take my hand, but he was the one who was alarmed. An ugly and bleeding kind of blister on my right index finger had been oozing for days. He wanted to know if I had ever had anything like it before, and I told him, yes, but never as severe.

Within a few minutes, he had connected me to a fine dermatologist across the Bay in San Francisco attached to the university hospital there. I went to see him the next day. He was very alarmed and ordered a "punch" biopsy, which hurt more than I can explain to this day. More than thirty years later, I can still make out the scar on that finger. The results came back; they were unclear, but there was probably something seriously wrong with me. He wanted to put me on massive steroids. I refused.

Then, all hell broke loose.

I had raging high fevers, bone-crunching pain, more of

the same ugly and bloody companions to my finger appeared in places all over my body. Now, they were called something official: "lesions." I couldn't walk, I couldn't move, I really could not function at all. My entire body was throbbing, and what wasn't throbbing was oozing or dripping blood.

I was a sight to behold. I was falling to bits in the most horrifying and ugly manner possible. It was something I had never envisioned in my worst nightmares of what might happen to me in my life with chronic disease.

Two weeks after I had resolutely refused those steroids, I was in the hospital, surrounded by teams of doctors from at least four distinct disciplines of medicine. There was talk of diseases I had never heard about before. Practically every afternoon, a new doctor opined with pompous sincerity and apology that I was "wickedly sick" "in grave crisis," or "seriously ill," and so forth, in an apparent attempt to secure my trust. Then each would give me his diagnosis. Not one of them matched the diagnosis of the previous doctor.

It was finally the dermatologist who intervened and took control; he had me placed under the care of the senior head of the division of rheumatology. This meant most of the time I was seen by his senior head resident, and not by him. The rheumatologists and the dermatologist, finally then, came to like to use the following words when talking to me: "atypical mixed connective tissue disease."

It didn't sound all that bad to me. It did not sound like a condition that was necessarily permanent. Maybe it was the word "mixed" that confused me. Unexpectedly, the body-mind-guru-doctor-shrink drove across the bay from Berkeley to the edges of San Francisco and walked into my hospital room. I remember thinking he would be angry because I had flunked all his mind-body tests. I thought I was in for a bad session with him. I had so misjudged him. He sat next to my bed for a very long time, and said to me that none of the doctors really knew what they were doing, because that was the nature of these sorts of diseases.

He hated to say it, but I had to take the steroids because my life had to be saved, which was the main issue and the only one that had to be dealt with immediately. He warned me against taking any diagnosis too seriously. He warned me about a life on steroids, but in a practical and medical way, not in a judgmental way. He reminded me about meditation practice and diet and finding an inner peace. In short, his message was this: "You are not to blame." His other message to me, plainly stated, was that it was unfair and I didn't deserve this. This remark was the very best medicine I got while I was in the hospital.

I didn't ask him if I would ever be completely well again and stay well forever. He probably believed I would be, for that was his brand of medical religion. Of course, I don't know what he actually thought. Would he have said the words "curtailment" or "remission" or would he have said the word "cure"? I never gave him the chance; I still wasn't anywhere close to the place where I would end up going. I had not yet begun the transformation that would lead me to become the woman who would write the words I have written in an earlier chapter of this book. "I am a person with chronic disease."

What he did was to reinforce this healing truth: that it was my body, and not me, the person, that was responsible.

In these later decades, many practitioners of alternative medicine have gone way out to the place of blame and shame. In so doing, they have greatly harmed many who are chronically ill. They have harmed us psychologically and have caused some of us to delay urgently needed medical intervention.

My doctor-guru-shrink was a different breed entirely. He is the only person I have met who caused me to give some serious thought to the possibility of reincarnation. He might well have been someone of great antiquity, who possessed an even deeper wisdom. Although he did nothing, in the end, to alleviate my physical suffering from illness, he took the first enormous blame boulder off my chest. For that, I remain forever in his debt. When I recall him, his presence floats into my mind as the softest sweetness, from a life's journey that has been anything and everything but that. I am sure he was somewhere in the back of mind, that day when I saw the article in Michael's office about "witchcraft and lupus."

The first years in New York were largely a replication of the same situations I had experienced in Berkeley. There would be flares. There would be extreme episodes. There would be more hospitalizations. There would be medications I hated—the regime of The Bitter Pill. However, I felt totally safe from medical harm, because by that point Michael was solely in charge of my situation, and, in our first meeting, in that collaborative style of his he told me we were a team. Yet, I still thought I would wake up one day to find the disease was gone. I would be able to wear it out and down, before it wore me out and down, or I would "grow out of it." I now realize what a naïve thought that was for a woman of both achievement and substance, fast approaching thirty.

Then, all of a sudden, in fact, it did what I had dreamed: it went away. Magic! Gone! Poof! Quite clearly, the fairy godmother had come in during a dream, and said to me, "Alida, now you will be well forever." Months and months went by and there was not even a trace of disease and then, more months, and then, I made it an entire year—well and drug free. I was out of jail! I thought for the first time since before I was twelve what a life without disease would mean for me. I realized I had been in deep denial since childhood. I had always assumed it would never go away; I had simply refused to articulate it to myself or anyone else.

One beautiful autumn day I had lunch with a colleague, whose husband was doing an advanced residency at the cancer hospital across from where Michael practices and conducts his research. I had dined at my friend's apartment, and because it was such a fine day, I decided to walk home. I saw Michael, about to cross the street to go to his side of "hospital row." I called out his name, formally, of course, in public, "Dr. Lockshin, it's me. It's Alida." He came toward me and greeted me warmly. I remember that he said I looked wonderful and that he was happy he hadn't seen me for so long. We had not yet become close social friends. I said to him, in words that still scream in my ears from time to time. "It is gone. It is absolutely gone. It's gone. I'm finished with it."

He looked at me and smiled and said something I thought at the time was strangely formal and a bit cold. He said, "Well, yes, they do that, they do that sometimes."

He meant the word "they" to represent diseases like mine. I was insistent. I said, no, it was gone. Nothing, no joint pain, no fever, skin as smooth and perfect as it could be—couldn't he see that? He smiled. We exchanged social tidbits; we each went on our way. His response had wounded me a tiny bit. I know all too well now, of course, why he could not ethically or realistically share my euphoria. Hope is undoubtedly what he felt that autumn afternoon, but not euphoria, and not positive elation. It would have been, for him, contrary to the facts of his experience.

Less than two months later, I felt strangely weak and rapidly started to lose a great amount of weight. I was working very hard and spending long hours finishing a large book based on some of the research studies I had conducted while still based at University of California, Berkeley. Colleagues and friends noted that I was pale, and expressed concern. Was I eating? Was I resting? I felt exhausted, but I was writing many hours a day, dashing to the Columbia University computer center sometimes at night to run data, and holding down a full time job as a program director in a foundation. (These were the prehistoric days before a laptop could run more than a university's entire mainframe system.) I did not take anyone's remarks seriously. After all, I was symptom free, wasn't I?

Then in California, the week before the Christmas holiday, I was upstairs in my parents' home and felt dizzy and suddenly weak. A hot rush came into my throat without warning. I thought I was going to vomit. I ran into the bathroom, and shut the door, and then I began to cough, in fact I began to choke. Large ugly looking things came out of my mouth from what I thought was my throat. They looked a little too similar to the old lesions of my fingers and elbows. Then, I started to spit up bright red fresh blood.

Denial was over forever. The disease was back and whatever it was now, was something it had not been before, and I was in for a rough ride, and I knew it. I wasn't in panic, or even in much fear. At that moment, the overwhelming feeling I had was unbearable sadness. Total grief. It had outsmarted me. It would take the lead and it would decide. I knew that my life would never be quite the same. Chronic illness was in the process of moving from a footnote to text. I called Michael at his home number. I told him what was going on and said that I would finish my short holiday visiting my parents, and a few friends in Southern California, but I would not go to Berkeley. I would cut the trip short by about a week or so. I finished by announcing I would report in to him as soon as I got back to New York.

This would not be a time for any doctor-patient collaboration, however. There was no negotiation and not much conversation. He told me to get on the next flight out of Los Angeles. And so I did.

Before the remission had taken me into a fantasy world, I had begun to worry about the "mixed connective tissue disease" diagnosis. I wondered what sort of disease it would turn out to be, ultimately. I thought it might well be lupus, so I worried often if it would hit my kidneys. My lungs?—Never thought about them and never worried about them betraying me. Once back in New York, I quickly learned I had a large lesion in my left lung. Cancer? I had never smoked in my life. However, it was considered a possibility, because the lesion had "fingers" attached to it. Nobody liked its shape too much. Quickly, however, a new term came into my sphere and has so remained as part of my life. *Wegener's granulomatosis.* I had a somewhat older (but not that all out of date) copy of the *Merck Manual.* I looked up the term, the description began: "Wegener's granulomatosis is a uniformly fatal disease…"

I closed the book and called two close friends at the time—a distinguished psychiatrist and his wife, an accomplished and celebrated editor of non-fiction books. They both came over. I asked him what he knew about Wegener's. He said I did not want to have that disease. I told him it looked like I might have that disease. They, along with their two sons, were a family of choice for the first many years of my existence in New York. They were a primary part of my main support system, outside of the medical team, during this crisis.

The next many months are a blur to me. There was a surgery. The thoracic surgeon, while very accomplished, was from a rigidly traditional male culture. He was Japanese, and refused to talk to me about the surgery without my husband or my brother or my boyfriend present to ask relevant questions. I said, "But you are going to operate on *me*, not on a man." He would not have it; I would have produced one of the men on his approved-of list if I had such in my life, but I had no one in those categories to fit the bill. Additionally, I was totally insulted by his approach. However, my friend, the psychiatrist, also on staff at the same hospital, came and sat in my room, and posed as my older brother.

I disliked the surgeon, he said things like, "Well, on Monday morning we are going to the church and we are going to get married." This was his way of talking about cracking open my chest and doing far more than I wanted to know about. It was just his style. It wasn't about his competence. It wasn't about his compassion, but I couldn't stand his manner and I could not relax around him. We did not and could not communicate. I was in despair.

The night before the surgery, a Sunday night, Michael came into my room very late. He said, "I've got some very good news. I just read Dr. X's notes in your file. His handwriting is very neat." It was the perfect form of reassurance I needed, and we both laughed. I think now Michael and I both needed to laugh. Dr. X, the surgeon, thought it might well be cancer. When it was not, but when the diagnosis was, in fact, the dreaded W, with something called *necrotizing vasculitis* now attached to it as well, Dr. X wanted me removed from his section of the hospital complex. He cured people. He was a surgeon. He did not want someone on his wing with a lingering and chronic illness that would not go away. He could not deal with a disease he could not take his scalpel to, and artfully carve away, forever. That is why he chose to be a surgeon and why Michael was chosen to be something other.

The disease spread quickly to the right lung. This caused one of my most darkly witty friends to say, "you don't have a 'right' lung, and so, what you mean is that now it is in the other lung too." I was in and out of the hospital. The Wegener's was having the time of its life. I couldn't tolerate the first drug; it gave me chemical hepatitis. It was a nightmare. It was the high drama of chronic illness. I assumed I was singing the ending aria of an opera just before everyone gets killed or dies and the curtain comes down.

I was wrong. I got better from the grave crisis, but not from the chronic Wegener's. This is the truth of the story of the *new katun*—it is a story, that most of the time is boring and depleting in its stubborn tenacity. However, it is rarely as dramatic as this on a regular basis, or we would die more efficiently and quickly, or get better and stay better.

The life-threatening times come, and then they go away, and then you must brace yourself. You do not brace yourself for the next horrific death-defying moment. Instead, what you must brace yourself for is the day-in-day-out wear and tear of it. What really hallmarks a life successfully lived with chronic disease is your ability to keep soldiering through. The bitter pill is that it is always just a little there, or a great deal there, but the unpleasant taste remains, in your mouth, in your routines, in your soul, and that is the fight we are engaged in for the long haul. We must not become overwhelmed by the exhaustion of it and the fear of the possible next grave crisis.

I became a fan of Flannery O'Connor's short stories when I was in high school. She had already died by then. At that point, I did not know that she had died of lupus. She had written her fiction throughout the darkness of her chronic and painful form of this disease, until almost her last days.

When she could no longer summon the strength to write or edit her fiction, she found the focus to write her friends, including some who were also sick, but with things less serious than lupus. She never whined. But, she did speak the truth about her fatigue and pain, and she always spoke of the lupus, in her letters, as something outside of her identity. It was always "her lupus," no question about that. But she was always Flannery, writer, friend, daughter, not lupus, with a-small-caps-flannery attached to the disease as if she were a footnote.

The life was Flannery's to live; and live it she did. Unfortunately it included this very nasty disease, which she would not be able to overcome and triumphantly out live into her old age. However, until the last half-coherent letter she wrote, her life is full testimony to one that did triumph over being defined by disease. I would say her writing even trumped the lupus itself, despite the fact the disease took her away far too soon.

By the time her collected letters came into my awareness, I was well into my new *katun*. I read them again as I prepared to think about this collaboration with Michael. I thought I might call this chapter *The Habit of Being* which is also the title of her volume of letters. It is a title selected by her good friend and the editor of the volume, Sally Fitzgerald. In her introduction she says she felt Flannery understood the habit of living, of being, the way that Flannery understood the work of Jacques Maritain in his *Art and Scholasticism*. Fitzgerald, remembering her beloved friend, wrote:

"Flannery consciously sought to attain to the habit of art, and did, by customary exercise and use, acquire it in the making of her novels and her stories. Less deliberately perhaps, and only in the course of living in accordance with her formative beliefs, as she consciously and profoundly wished to do, she acquired as well, I think, a second distinguished habit which I have called 'the habit of being': an excellence not only of action but of interior disposition and activity that increasingly reflected the object, the being, which specified it, and was itself reflected in what she did and said."

When I read again the Fitzgerald introduction and then the Flannery O'Connor letters, especially the last ones, I knew I would call this chapter, "The Bitter Pill." First, I have had to swallow the bitter pill of acceptance of this new *katun*, and then, hopefully I have worked hard, and must continue to do so, to attain the goal all of us hope to achieve, ill or well—to be able to compose for myself a life of meaning and of worth. It takes a great deal of habituated use to grow accustomed to the taste of the bitter pill, but it is only after that, that it becomes possible to devote the time needed to perfect a much better, and far more important habit…"the habit of being…."

AB

A Weak Spot

Alida told me that I do not know my patients' secrets. Doctors know, she said, only what their patients choose to show, and not how secrets define more important parts of their lives

She raises an interesting point. So doctors do not know the effects of love or loss? Or of other secrets that patients keep? I hope it is not true.

But maybe she is right. When I first heard what she said I thought: Bingo. Alida put her finger on a weak spot—one that is, however, both weaker and stronger than she knows.

The strength is that I do know something about the process of secrets, or at least I think I do. The weakness is that I do not know either their content or their intensity. Another weakness: if I am unduly confident that I know my patient, I can be startlingly surprised.

For example, the secret of love. I know a little bit about this need. I see young women…. I see young women bringing their young men to me. I talk to fiancés. I hear what women say when they ask me about marriage, pregnancy, and children. Sometimes I see in their fiancés' eyes (I suspect they do not) hesitation or insincerity. The women do not ask me to judge their men, nor would I if they did. Instead I ignore the furtive glances, offer congratulations and advice, while fearing the day this woman's mate will leave and she will return in tears.

To be sure, some marriages and relationships do hold, and some appear to hold because a fortune would be out of reach if the relationship were to dissolve. And sometimes I see real love. Alida is right. I do know about the process, I know longing is there, but I know very little more. The details are beyond my ken.

That is, until someone opens my eyes. I, the visitor to the land of the chronically ill, am sometimes invited in. I anticipate one thing; another happens. I am unprepared, then a window opens. I catch a brief glimpse of this hidden world, and am surprised by what I see.

The woman entered my life through an urgent, desperate telephone call. She was in an intensive care unit at a small local hospital and was catastrophically ill. Her distraught husband had learned my name, was persistent, broke through my office barriers, and got me on the phone. He requested that she be transferred to our hospital. From the description of his wife—tracheotomy and ventilator, kidneys failing, several strokes, seizures, all having occurred within a very few days—it was inconceivable that we could accept a transfer; she was too unstable and too ill. That afternoon I spoke to the husband for a long time. When she was stable to move, I said, if she survived this crisis (I didn't tell him that I doubted she would), we could consider a transfer, but not just now.

She did survive and she did come under my care. I do not know—cannot know—what she had been like when she was a new bride a decade before, or five years ago, or even one. But now, and for the next eight years, this woman was demented and infantile, as a result of her several strokes. She could carry on a superficially coherent conversation, when she was not under duress, so long as no deep thought was required. "How do you feel? What did you do yesterday?" Those sorts of things. But ask her something substantive and she would become quite confused. If her world were perturbed——undergoing a minor medical procedure, for instance—she became a two-year-old, screaming hysterically, calling for her parents, irrational, uncontrollable, until the period of stress passed by.

They had no children. Her husband was a printer who owned his own shop and was able to set his working hours. He took her to his shop, gave her pretend paper work, and made a great effort to keep her comfortable and at his side. At other times her parents stayed with her at home. Easily confused, likely to become lost, she was never left alone.

As expected, her kidneys slowly failed. Because of the needles and the procedures that would ensue, she refused dialysis when the first symptoms of kidney failure came. Eventually she developed nausea and vomiting, as patients with kidney failure do. She then did allow dialysis. In one sense this was good because her overall health improved, but she lived a distance away from our hospital and was assigned to an outpatient dialysis facility near her home. This assignment placed her in the hands of different doctors, in unfamiliar places, unsettling enough when a brain is intact, quite disturbing to someone who is always confused.

Bad brain function and kidney failure make a poor match. Every perturbance, every bump in the road turned into: "I want my mommy," tireless screaming, and, to her husband, unexpectedly, repeatedly and persistently, "Who are you? You never did anything for me!" She told him to go away. She cried out in terror when he came near. The doctors at the outpatient facility called us for help time and time again.

After a year or so of trying to take care of her, a year of frightening her when he came near, her husband let her parents take charge. Old, not perceptive, lacking subtlety, the parents concluded that he had done something awful to her (I very much doubt this was so) and they cut off contact with him. For news about her he depended on intermediaries, including me. Now the parents called me repeatedly when she was hysterical, and I, literally in *loco parentis,* would talk to her by telephone, tell her to take deep breaths, to stop crying, to tell me what was wrong, and she would calm down. Her husband would call me from time to time to ask about her.

This went on for another year, a crisis every month or so, until one day her father called to tell me that she had been found to have a high fever when she showed up for dialysis, that pneumonia had been diagnosed, and that she had been taken to a hospital near her home. The next day or the day after that her father called to say that she had died. Infections in dialysis patients—particularly demented ones who do not report symptoms very well—are very serious so I was not surprised. I tried to call the husband, but it turned out that I did not have his new, unlisted telephone number and I could not call.

He heard about her death a week or two after that. Not knowing about his father-in-law's call to me, he wanted me to know that she had died. "They didn't even tell me," he said. "I just found out today." He had only learned the news in the course of making one of his regular calls to a mutual friend. I told him that I had heard.

To my surprise, this manly man, this hardworking, quiet and competent man, paused and then began to sob. "I tried so hard," he said, and then said again, "Why did she turn against me? What did I do wrong?"

I had not been prepared for his call and even less for this response. This was one injury too much to bear, knowing his in-laws had informed me of his wife's death, and not him.

This was a second conversation that lasted a very long time. I gave him a figurative hug over the telephone line, and told him he had done more than most men could. I explained, although I don't know even today that he understood (we had had this conversation before), how damaged brains cause personalities to change and how, while the body may have looked the same, the woman he loved had been no longer there, and had not been for many years.

So Alida is probably right. There are patients' secrets that I am incompetent to share. For the years that I knew this couple I had no concept of the depth of his love or to what extent her brain damage had caused her emotional rejection of her husband. Visiting and inhabiting the land of chronic disease are two very different things. There are many parts of my patients' lives that I cannot know, unless and until I am invited in.

I do know that the lives of persons with chronic illness have voids both articulated and not, crevices and tunnels in the polar glaciers that complete the worlds of which their lives consist. Knowing that the voids exist is where my competence ends. To intuit the places of emptiness is the best that I can do. To sense its quality, to understand its depth, to comprehend its effect are skills that I can only pray to learn.

Patients do not often tell me, the somewhat distant older man standing before them, the person whose time they contracted for half an hour and to whom they pay a fee, things that are closest to their souls. They do not often volunteer thoughts not yet articulated, but which they may later come to understand, once prompted by my probing questions to greater self-awareness. It would take, I think, hours and weeks and months of conversation in a deeply intimate situation for someone to tell me what having to sit by and watch a loved one suffer does to a relationship or to one's hopes and dreams.

For my part, I cannot confidently read someone's unexpressed existential dread. I cannot intuit long past personal or family histories that place unimaginable specters in the deepest recesses of one's brain. Yet, I think that if I could understand these things I would better comprehend what my patient's illness means to her and her family and, perhaps, we would both profit by this exchange.

But these things may still be too much to know. Perhaps my attempting to comprehend these voids may transform my thought from the scientific to the mystical and thereby diminish my professional skill. Perhaps not knowing makes my judgment less confused and more lucid. Perhaps it is enough to know that these voids exist and maybe, just maybe, the patient and the doctor, the doctor and the patient, together can on occasion carry a lantern powerful enough, albeit dimly, to illuminate the depths.

MDL

Love and Loss

Alan Pakula directed a film in the early 1970's that slipped by most people, despite many excellent reviews. Titled *Love and Pain and The Whole Damn Thing,* it stars Maggie Smith, luminescent, funny and heartbreaking in her determination to maintain her dignity, despite her obvious yearning for solitude and a suspicious urgency to her manner.

Smith plays an eccentric, unmarried English woman with a secret, the nature of which is no mystery to anyone holding a passport to my country: she is on a pre-exit adventure, before she succumbs to a chronic and unspecified illness. In my mind, it just had to be lupus. The storyline has a twist that stung me when I first saw the film. In retrospect, I am glad I am not viewing it now for the first time, because it would undoubtedly shatter me.

The leading boy-man was the young Timothy Bottoms, playing the hapless son of a famous professor, asthmatic and socially awkward, who has signed on for a tour through Spain to "find himself." Bottoms and Smith accidentally end up as seatmates on the tour bus, become enchanted with one another, and ultimately, become lovers.

I was about the same age as Bottoms when I first saw the movie. The notion that he could find a middle-age woman so sensually attractive seemed silly to me. In my twenties, I had entered the height of whatever would qualify for my youthful beauty. Now, in middle age, in a season of illness, I no longer find that part of the film the fairy-tale. I understand that a much younger man could love a woman entering the dusk of her beauty. Quite unexpectedly, I had that moment in my life when I was fortunate enough to experience a profound connection to an extraordinary younger man. I would call that experience love; I believe he did as well.

What seems to me the fantasy of the movie lies in the notion that anyone, at any age, at any time—would choose to hang in there with a chronically ill person. In my experience, people aren't good at handling the roller coaster-like experience of a loved one's chronic disease. Even those who say they can do it, the ones who insist they can hold the ground with you, and help you fight back, often can't. They somehow find a totally extraneous, and often petty, reason to assign you to the dumpster.

In the movie, Smith feebly attempts to dismiss Bottoms from her life and send him on his youthful way. Instead he refuses to go away, telling her life itself is about "love and pain, and the whole damn thing." When we were watching the film, my husband had already experienced at least two of my hospitalizations. Despite his insistence he would always be there with me, even if my disease came back in full force, I knew that would not be the case.

I watched Timothy Bottoms with the ill, but elegantly brave, Maggie Smith go off together toward a shortened, albeit happy horizon. I understood my own story would be a quite different one.

I knew the beautiful young man sitting next to me in the cinema, my supposed life's companion, would not be there forever. When the going got scary and the suffering seemingly endless, we would not be holding hands, fighting back his fears, and my pain. When we met I was in total remission. But, I was in anything but remission at the time we were watching Maggie and Timothy trying to figure life out on the silver screen. I knew our future would not include a sunset, complete with accompanying Hollywood orchestration.

And I was right. My husband did leave me. His exit would

occur after yet another hospitalization of mine. He gave lots of reasons that were about anything and everything else; in fact, he wanted out because I was sick too often. It was our unspoken truth. Nonetheless, we pretended that my chronic illness had nothing to do with the termination of our relationship. He delivered sermons to me about why he had to leave. They seemed almost flattering, perhaps even kind, at the time; they seem like something else entirely now.

He said, among many other things, that our marriage was "just weird enough to have a divorce in the middle of it." During one of his speeches, I fought the temptation to attach myself to his ankle, but pride and a fierce feminism kept me from doing that. That's a lie: pride and feminism notwithstanding, the only reason I didn't beg him to stay was because I knew that it would be futile. The certainty of this was the only thing that saved me from further humiliation.

He was my safety net. I thought of him as my reward for having survived a childhood hell. He was my consolation for those sorrows. He was, as if, from the old Yiddish saying: "from many, many, many woes, comes one great consolation."

We appeared to be a good, if not a perfect, match. Members of the family called us "the gazelles" because we were tall and lean, and moved through time and space together in quick delight. When I looked into his eyes I thought they sparkled with words that said: "Everything is fine; you are home." Yet, our life together would not have a Hollywood ending. If it had been a movie, it would have bombed at the box office. In an exit remark, he told me how valiant I always was during my illnesses.

He once told me he thought of us as artists, painting side-by-side on a beautiful beach. In his daydreams, I had a large canvas spread out, and was working on what he referred to as a magnificently colorful painting. He saw himself standing next to me, with an easel, and a small stretched canvas, making an intricate pen and ink drawing. In his mind, everyone stopped to admire my painting. I had all the admirers; he was all but invisible. That was how he saw life with me.

Decades later, this comment remains unforgettable: "I don't always want to be in the shadow of your brilliant and colorful personality." He was certainly the more accomplished of us, at that point, and by far the more recognized professionally. His intellectual currency had much more worth than mine. I don't believe he felt eclipsed by my flamboyance. He had enjoyed my energy enormously before I had become ill again. As a serious scientist, he often commented he lived inside his head too much, and that I lived in a world of literature and words and life and politics. He loved the way I bore him along on a wake of conversation and adventures. It was his major attraction to me, from the instant we met. His leaving was about something else—something quite apart from divergent personality styles.

I believe he felt stalked by the shadow of my illness. He was afraid of what might happen to me in the near or distant future. He was unhappy that I was so fearful of pregnancy, of motherhood. His commitment to the ethics of his childhood upbringing, coupled with his family's devotion to me, essentially forbade him from abandoning a sick wife.

Therefore, to salvage the sense of his own integrity and preserve his self-esteem, as well as to maintain his dignity within the family as the eldest son—he had to come up with a more acceptable scenario. An overpowering wife was a justifiable reason to leave a marriage; an overpowering disease was not.

When we were watching the movie, our ending scene was

still some years in the future. During the time it took for the reel to spin through the projector and onto the screen, and simultaneously into the memory bank of my brain's own film library, I understood a profound truth: I knew that whenever my last *katun* was about to elapse, it would not be with this man holding me close to him.

I knew that before it had happened, before there was a whisper of this. How did I know it with such certainty then? Why was I so sure that when I was approximately the age Maggie Smith was made up to be in the film, winding down from a lifetime of tenacious and rare autoimmune illness, the man sitting next to me in that theater would not be trotting around my last lap with me? Some might call it having a sixth sense. I call it a highly tuned "seventh" sense that those of us with chronic diseases often develop rapidly, along with the progression of our diseases.

My dear friend and mentor, the late Dr. Samuel Bloom, wrote a book entitled *Word As Scalpel*. Sam Bloom was a leader in the development of the field that has come to be known as "medical sociology." He pioneered research involving doctors and social scientists working in teams, in order to come to a better understanding of the intersection of medicine, patients and community. The quote that he used as his title refers to the ability a doctor possesses to "cut" a patient just as deeply as a scalpel simply by using the wrong words. So, too can a lover, spouse or partner cut into the soul of a chronically ill person. Harsh words are aimed, sometimes in fear, sometimes in anger at the disease and its intrusion on a loved one, or on their lives in general. Words can be destructive weapons. Their impact can last an entire lifetime.

At some point prior to my husband's departure from my life, I overheard him talking to one of his best friends. We were then enmeshed in a tragic moment: this friend's wife, also a dear friend of mine—a young and gifted woman and the mother of three small children—was dying of a benign, but inoperable, brain tumor. As she was entering the last stages of her life, I was inconveniently in and out of the hospital as well with flare-ups of my own condition.

Amidst the discussion and tears of despair in the room next door, though I was only half listening to their conversation, I heard my husband utter the sentence that still haunts me. During a pause in his anguished grieving, our friend concluded that nobody really could understand what it was like for him and their three children to lose a young wife and mother. I then heard my husband's own unmistakable voice, as it is engraved in my heart, presumably to serve as future warning to self: "Yes, it's true, but look at my situation. At least, she has the good grace to die."

At last, the shoe had finally dropped, but it was more like a large combat boot. All my fears were encapsulated in this one sentence. I had become a burden. It was impossible for him to cope with me, my disease, with the effects of the drugs I was taking. I needed to get out of his way. I really ought to die, too. At least, that is what it felt like to me then. I don't think he meant it to be as cruel as it sounds, especially when it is written down and read aloud. But, it is certainly the case that he was burned out on me, and on my disease.

Not long after we had buried our friend, my husband left me forever. In one of the last letters to me while we were still trying to salvage our marriage, he wrote, "I am sorry, but I guess I am all healed out with you." I was too stricken by losing him, and too sick at the time, to understand he had delivered into the hands of my more ferocious feminist sisters a handy verbal weapon which they then used in an attempt to make me laugh. After I had told them these words of his, that he was just "all healed out," I discovered a mysterious card taped to my refrigerator door with the following neatly typed: "Time Wounds All Heels."

Everyone thought it was funny. Some of my friends thought it was absolutely hilarious. I did not think it was so funny; I did not think anything at all was funny, or ever would be again. But, I do now. Entering the last segment of my final *katun*, I can't imagine I'll want, or God knows, trust, that a much younger man, or any man at all, will be keeping time with me. Accepting this reality is far more difficult than adjusting to the constant presence of chronic disease. The absence of a supportive life's companion is much harder for me to come to grips with than the inevitability of what the course of my illness, and the immunosuppressive drugs, have done, and will continue to do, to my body. For me, it has been the toughest lesson I have had to learn.

Some years later, I threw caution to the winds and again permitted myself to experience love with a man I trusted. This love, however, was not dictated by youth, but fueled by an eerie intellectual compatibility. I thought, here was a man with an almost inexpressible brilliance, range of thought, expanse of ideas and passion. He forced me to think more complexly, to take on more demanding and involving projects. He had compassion for me, and a tenderness he exhibited at the same time as he confronted my illness head-on, or so it seemed.

At first, I tried to keep him in the dark about what might happen to me, but he felt insulted and asked that I not infantilize him. He insisted that he wanted to be part of the process, not apart from it. His feelings took me by storm. Because we had been friends, he was able to infiltrate the barbed wire of my personal defense system. I suspended my cautious, often suspicious stance.

As if in a fantasy, he came into my life in ways that were indeed real. For a time, he represented the kind of man I had only dreamed existed. He reminded me how strong I was, and that I could handle just about anything. Yet, he also helped me when I found I really couldn't do everything alone. Once, during a trip, when I essentially collapsed with fatigue from fighting the illness, he was there, on all levels, and in all ways.

Suddenly, the return of illness threw me off course, both physically and emotionally. Its full-blown appearance without enough warning clearly stunned him. Initially, however, I wasn't worried. He was such a manly man; I knew he could handle it. I understood and had witnessed both his strength of character and his competence in many areas. So much did I believe in his ability to support me emotionally, that I took off my Warrior Woman's costume, and put down my shield and sword. I did so with the full confidence that he could and would cope during a crisis. And, I simply did not have the energy to perform acts of false bravado and independence.

His response, however, to a serious health crisis during our relationship devastated me. First, he asserted that there had never been anything at all between us. Then, when I was terrified and became frantic, he completely closed me out of his life. He would not respond to any form of communication I attempted. He was furious! I felt he was treating me as if I were a naughty child who had grievously misbehaved. He had cast himself into the role of the stern and dictatorial parent, who would alone decide on our future together. I had reached out to him when I had been running an exceedingly high fever, and was quite incoherent. My illness and a drug interaction had taken me to the edge. I had so needed him in that passage. We tried to patch it up; I attempted to make a joke about being sent to "Relationship-Siberia." He retaliated with a list of all the things he most disliked about me, and finished with a sweeping statement about how it would never have worked out in any event.

What he did was cruel, but had a logical, if horrifying, coherence. It was also oddly familiar. The things he had loved about me—how I had amused him, the times we had enjoyed together—everything had been turned around and reinterpreted. He was not, of course, giving up on us because I was so ill. He did not want to see me any longer because I was absolutely impossible.

I recognized the place he had taken himself and I knew he would refuse to budge from the protective fortress he had built around himself. It was a series of behaviors with harsher manners that I recognized from a not completely faded memory of my past. The fact that I had seen clearly and immediately the termination of our time together made it much worse and more painful for me to endure.

In her last book, entitled, *Maybe,* Lillian Hellman wrote "… but recovery is not the word. You can't recover from what you do not understand." Perhaps she was right, or should I say "maybe"? But, in this instance I could not recover easily because I understood it all far too well. I have not chosen to risk this magnitude of loss again. I will not risk it, because I must not risk it.

It is distressing to accept the loss of a person one has felt so deeply about, and an aching exercise in reality-therapy to remind myself that I will not be able to love fully or to be loved in turn. The end of love is never easy. For anyone, man or woman, who has permitted him or herself to trust, the withdrawal of love with its attendant support and compassion is a threat.

I will not allow myself to trust again at this level of

confidence and belief; it is too great a risk. It is however, a risk my healthy friends can take if they choose. But, it is an option that the woman inside me must decline for the wellbeing of the patient inside me. The woman steps aside, quite reluctantly, for the patient, and in so doing, the woman-self admits that the patient-self knows better than to exercise the option, although the woman-self would consider it. However, both the woman and the patient, who co-exist inside the being called Alida, know it is too big a gamble. If I were to love again, and lose again, would I have willingly and purposefully put myself in peril?

I am not alone. Those who are chronically ill lose out more often than attain enduring love. That is a sad, but honest statement. If we are keen on survival, sometimes we must avoid the opportunity to take the risks with relationships that others can afford to take. While others brave serious heartbreak, or a poetic form of it, which I have called in other writings by the term "heartgrief," we endure much more.

We open ourselves to the unraveling of the entire, often badly taped-together package of our physically and emotionally damaged selves. In all the losses one experiences in a life so rudely interrupted by disease, it is that of a hope of lasting, compassionate and tender love that wounds in ways which can never be described in medical terms.

The Israeli poet Yehuda Amichai's last book of poems, written as he knew he was dying, *Open/Closed/Open,* includes a poem that has become my prayer for strength and for personal understanding. It is entitled *The Precision of Pain and the Blurriness of Joy: The Touch of Longing is Everywhere.* It contains 16 stanzas, but it is to the last one, "16," I return frequently:

"The precision of pain and the blurriness of joy. I'm thinking how precise people are when they describe their pain in a doctor's office. Even those who haven't learned to read and write are precise: this one is a throbbing pain, that one's a wrenching pain, this one gnaws, that one burns, this is a sharp pain and that, a dull one. Right here. Precisely here, yes, yes.' Joy blurs everything. I've heard people say after nights of love and feasting, 'It was great, I was in seventh heaven.' Even the spaceman who floated in outer space, tethered to a spaceship could say only, 'Great, wonderful, I have no words.'
The blurriness of joy and the precision of pain—I want to describe with a sharp pain's precision, happiness and blurry joy. I learned to speak among the pains."

For those of us who are seeking and searching the need to curb the longing for that blurriness of joy, our most challenging assignment is "to speak among the pains." This is the key to our survival. If we are not extremely cautious and instead cling to unrealistic romantic fantasies, we can find ourselves in dangerous terrain. If I were to become Czar of All Chronically Ill Patients, I would demand that patients and doctors come together to find a way to approach this delicate and awkward topic in their private dialogues and perhaps even in public ones.

Of the many sacrifices I have sustained in this life the biggest by far is the realization that I am not entitled to experience happiness with another person in a loving relationship. Letting go of this presumed normal human entitlement is the heaviest thing I have had to cast aside, as I have attempted to unburden myself and live as well as I can, while still coping with lifelong disease.

Yet, it has proven impossible for me to even begin to

have a frank and open conversation with Michael on this topic. Even after all these years, it feels humiliating, and makes me feel too vulnerable. As I write the details of these most intimate experiences I have lived through, I know that Michael, who knows a great deal about me, does not know my defining secrets. If he suspects, he has only a vague notion of its intense effect on me, and what it does to my motivation to fight back.

I wonder if it would have mattered in treatment discussions—or, in questions, perhaps, of why one does or doesn't have a remission. I also wonder if my honesty might have added anything to the ongoing dialogue of the dynamics of chronic disease itself. Yet, I have never been able to invite him into this part of my world. We speak in general terms about the difficulty of intimacy and illness, but I have never been able to cross into these secrets of my heartgrief.

I do believe that this topic—the loss of love and the loss of a hope for love—is an aspect of chronic illness that should be addressed in our mutual struggle to combat and limit the devastation that occurs during the journey. Perhaps I have not spoken of it because I am ashamed I allowed this to cause me additional pain, when I have so much random physical pain present virtually every single day of my life. In the end, I probably withheld these things because I feel I failed Michael by allowing the risky business of love to intrude into an already compromised life, when he has worked so hard to keep me as functional as I am.

There is an ongoing internal debate about what to disclose about our health status, and when to disclose what is going on, even to a spouse or life-long partner or companion. Are we banks? Must we always engage in full-disclosure? I've done it both ways. I have hidden the illness, even when it has been somewhat active or moderately "hot." I've used various ploys and disguises, including wit and humor. I've chosen the full disclosure route as well, rarely, but when I do it goes something like: "Here it is. Here is what I have gone through and what you might have to face if you are with me."

My approaches, or my decisions, the one, to hide or the other, to disclose, have never worked well for me; perhaps this is because I have always been ill. Perhaps it is different for those who have been in long established or committed relationships. Maybe they are more successful in the approaches they use with their companions or spouses or lovers, who become active members of the team, and not merely part of a coping strategy or yet another management issue for the sick to deal with.

I was denied these possibilities, not because of social class, geographic location, education, age difference, faith or core belief systems. The man I loved had the luxury, indeed the entitlement, to feel his life might well spread across at least another three decades. He therefore had no patience because he could not comprehend or understand that at times I live rapidly and in the present tense. There are times when I make plans quickly. He was unable to decipher these behaviors as the codes they contained about my sense of time. I can now imagine that he would not have understood when I am often so methodical, even slow, in my work.

He could not know that at these times I feel "my wheel turning quickly"—too quickly—to borrow a phrase from Buddhist thought. He could not see that it was the turning of my wheel, which added to my urgent requirement to settle on schedules or plans. He saw instead, only inappropriate requests, which made him increasingly judgmental, irritable or angry.

I have had to come to terms with the fact that we faced something insurmountable that kept us from continuing on as the soul mates I had at the time believed we truly were. However, the time we spent together provided me with a powerful gift because it showed faith that I would choose to seek joy and contentment over hopelessness and fatalism.

In our shared trust of one another something transformative happened. I tasted the sweetness of courage that comes only when a significant other is holding your hand through a rough patch. The memory of that still survives in my soul. When I would think of him after his departure from my life, the reality of his absence highlighted the fact that I was completely alone with the "whole damn thing." Yet, it remains the case that for a miraculous moment or two I experienced what "normal" people often take for granted.

People like me hope to be loved in spite of our illness. We dream we might also be loved for our noble defiance of illness. We fantasize that we will find partners, lovers, companions or spouses who will be constant and loyal. We ask their forgiveness when symptoms or drugs make us less than we are, or more emotionally overwrought than we would choose. We all want someone, at any age, across the decades of our struggle to tell us: "Yes, I'm here with you. I'm not going anywhere. After all, life is love and pain and the whole damn thing." Most of us get an extra large serving of "the whole damn thing" to say nothing of a super-sized serving of the pain; but not enough of us get a generous portion of the love.

Those who do get the love and the faithful companionship of a significant other are able to gain entrance to a different part of our land. Those people have a special key to a safer place which in itself can be a healing tool. Hopefully, those who do receive that invaluable support from their partners find in themselves the ability to express their gratitude.

I believe it especially hard for a man to remain involved with a frequently unwell woman. I think one of the reasons is this: the afflicted partner does not die, at least all that quickly. It is assumed great heroism is involved when a partner stays close to a woman with cancer, until the last breath of her battle. I think it highly admirable, but frankly, I don't find this heroic. Virulent cancer has its own schedule. Plans can be made. Tragic though it may be, a partner can pace himself. With incurable chronic disease, on the other hand, due to its unpredictable nature, it is as if we are asking a spouse, a lover, a companion, to always be on call, on alert, at the ready.

Betty Friedan was one of the primary "mothers" of the post-suffrage, second wave of the women's movement. Her book *The Feminine Mystique* made her name, and the word feminism, synonymous. She was not only one of the founding mothers; she was a mother of choice for me and a dear, close friend. I did in fact think of her as another mother. I know she preferred to think of me as her young girlfriend. It didn't matter to me; our relationship worked throughout three decades, although given her exceedingly stormy personality, it wasn't without its troubles.

When she died, I wrote her obituary for the *Women's Media Center's* website. I was also asked by a number of other journalists for a quote. One sticks in my mind. When asked by a journalist how best to describe Betty's personal life, which was largely one of disappointment, I said simply: "Love eluded her."

Betty and I used to talk about our inability to connect to a man in the meaningful and authentically intimate ways we both longed to experience. She would say she was not going to find lasting love because of who she was and what she represented. Most men didn't want to cope with being the man attached to Betty Friedan. She candidly told me quite often I was unlikely to find the right companion and soul mate because of my illness. She was not a stranger to chronic illness herself, as she suffered with serious asthma for years. The kind of enduring love she dreamed of finding in her life did elude her, in fact, until her dying day.

It seems only appropriate to conclude a chapter on love and loss with Betty Friedan, and with my own views on gender and illness. I believe that gender plays a significant role in this discussion.

We still live in a world not unlike the one that Virginia Woolf described in *A Room of One's Own*. The external world is hard on men, as, of course, it is on women. It is difficult for women in different ways, but it is not a pure paradise for men, either. While we have entered a two-paycheck world, some women seek the man who is a "financial trophy" in somewhat the same demeaning way younger beautiful women are referred to as "arm-candy" for older men. In our "post-feminist" society, I often hear young women evaluating potential husbands or companions as commodities. How much do they earn? Where will they be able to live? Will they have a country house?

Woolf said important words about men, their fragility, and their needs. She said that in a world that was judgmental, competitive and demanding, men needed to believe in themselves completely before they left their homes in the morning, and that it was the women in their lives who provided a much-needed mirror that allowed the men to go forward in a harsh world. I am not sure this assumption of Woolf's has changed much—suffrage, equality, feminism and all the rest notwithstanding.

Chronic illness in a female partner gnaws at a man's sense

of control, his sense of power, his sense of being victorious against danger. Call it what you will, and if you wish, go ahead and accuse me of being politically incorrect. Whatever you want to label my remarks, it remains the case that a chronically ill woman threatens a man's sense of himself, and calls into question his feelings of success as a man, a lover, a "white knight."

Sometimes, we unwell women fall into the trap of wishing that they could rescue us, not from our lives or our jobs, but from our diseases. And, who could blame us? In the end, I can't be so judgmental and unforgiving that I am unable to find compassion in my heart for the men who just can't do it, even if they have so hurt us in their departures. Chronic disease robs us of our sense of ourselves, of our identity as attractive women, of our privacy and dignity; and in an ironic twist, our illnesses also dig away at a man's sense of his own maleness, in turn posing a threat to his core gender identity.

During the feminist movement, one of the things we used to chant in protest marches was: "the personal is political." I am not sure that turned out to be true, but what is true is that a woman's chronic illness becomes a fairly public struggle that a man whom she loves must also live through with her.

Most men, particularly those born before the feminist movement (baby boomer men being the largest number of this population) want to win. If their wives, their lovers, or companions aren't getting better, or are getting sicker, they question themselves whether it is somehow their fault. Did they cause it? Are they bad lovers, bad husbands, bad fathers? The self-blame begins, goes on, and then spins out of control.

For some men, when they can't "fix it" they feel they have to leave the relationship, sometimes abruptly. We don't, in fact, expect them to fix it. Most of the time what we have needed from them most desperately is a simple thing—that they hold us, just hold us, knowing full well neither of us can make the disease go away. This small act, and the reality of their physical presence, is heroic enough behavior for any of us who have been in this battle for any length of time.

At some juncture in the life of every chronically ill person, I suspect there comes a time when we blame ourselves. How did this happen to me? Am I somehow responsible for the emergence of my illness at the most inopportune times? If only I had handled myself better in that crisis. If only I had not been so afraid, and confessed how I was fearful I would not see him again. If only I had not been so ill from the chemotherapy, if only I had made that dinner party. If only I had not mentioned the fact I was in horrific pain. If only, if only, if only." When you get to the end of the IF ONLY ROAD, you find you have reached another road marked: DEAD-END. You can blame yourself all you want, but if you are alone, it isn't because you have done it completely wrong. It is because you have been betrayed by something not even the best teams of research doctors yet understand, and maybe never will.

What I say to my comrades in this battle is that when you find yourself alone for the first time, or alone again, or still alone, when your dreams have been shattered—when you have hit bottom and feel like a piece of discarded debris, try to remember this: before you hate the person who has left you, think about what it might have been like for them. Try to reach a higher place of acceptance, if not forgiveness.

If you despise yourself for an intemperate remark you made during an episode of illness, or fearing its return, if you are disgusted with yourself for not being able to curb an anxious or too needy demand or request, remind yourself of this: the path we walk is arduous and filled with boulders, ditches and canyons. Force yourself to say these words, even when you are not convinced you believe them: "I did the very best I could. I grieve the loss of this love and this relationship. But, I do not blame myself, for I truly did all I could at that moment, within the parameters of my illness."

The man who left me said something that has become somewhat of a personal mantra. In his anger at what he considered that inappropriate request and improper communication, he wrote, and then almost shouted at me: "This is from another planet." I was too ill, too weary, and too frightened to say what needed to be said to him: "Well, yes, of course, it is from a different planet. From time to time, I have to live there. I want to get off this planet and I will. But, first, do you think you could just wait it out with me?"

Instead, I apologized and asked that he not give up on us. I tried to calm him down and remind him of the things we had shared. As an adult woman, I did what I had refused steadfastly to do in my twenties. I tried to tie him down with me on this other planet until we could both be airlifted from its hideous landscape. I implored him to remember those things he liked about me the most. It was too late. He was gone: it was as if he had only been an apparition.

I deeply regretted how much of myself I had exposed to him and how honest I had been about my disease. Many of my deepest secrets went away with him—secrets I will never be able to retrieve. And even if I had been able to, it would not matter—they are not secrets any longer. As time passed, there was no real healing, but instead resignation to what had happened. The resignation eventually turned into a nagging throb of sorrow for what might have been, for both of us.

I no longer blame myself for being unable to cope alone,

in dread fear—for desiring the sound of his melodic voice. I do not blame him for being exasperated beyond his level of tolerance. I wish I had been able to feel at that time the compassion I feel for him now. In the end, however, we both did the best we could at that intense moment, when my disease took charge of our dialogue and, consequently, our relationship. We live with the threat of a series of symptoms returning, the recurrence of serious illness, flares, and drug side effects, any and all of which can throw a monkey wrench into our chance for happiness or take it away from us completely, without the courtesy of prior notification. And, we live with this set of fears and threats on a daily basis. By this point in my life, I can say I forgive the men who did not stay, as much as I forgive myself.

I offer my own prayers, secular and sacred, that future generations of women who are also assigned a life sentence with one variety of chronic disease or another (from the vast number of possible diagnoses) will face a less difficult world than that which I have faced and muddled through, mostly alone. My most passionately repeated prayers continue to be for the young girls who are, in this very instant as I write these words, experiencing the same pains and symptoms I did at their age. My dream is that they will emerge into their fifties and beyond, with stories more of health than illness, and more of love than loss.

AB

The Mirror and The Lens

Ah! To be unable to see oneself! A mirror! A mirror! A mirror! A mirror!

André Gide—*The Discourse of Narcissus*

It is a rather rude awakening, late in a career, to learn that others see oneself differently than one sees oneself. I had thought of myself as having fairly profound self-knowledge. Self-consciously introspective, I, to whom Proust was once a demi-god, and I, who as a youth, dutifully collated and filed self-affirming quotes from Valéry, Gide, and Rimbaud, am just now beginning to understand: the doctor whom Alida describes is not the person I believe myself to be. And, more important: I am hearing only a part of what she says.

I began to think about this flaw. I decided to retune my ear to learn how I could hear differently. I tried this the first week after the Christmas-New Year holidays. I listened and read differently at these points of contact: office visits, season's greeting cards, and emails. (Telephone calls are quite focused and do not easily lend themselves to digression.)

With my ear tuned to this different frequency, I heard patients say things that I had not heard—or had not melded with my understanding of their needs—before. I did not solicit any of the following quotes; they are spontaneous comments that I chose to record. The quotes are approximate. I wrote them down at the end of the day. I have grouped them into categories, and to improve clarity have indicated context in brackets.

The content of the comments speaks for itself. The quantity of the comments startled me. I recorded only a fraction of those I heard—in a short office week that consisted of only seventeen hours!

Almost every other patient, usually as an aside or as part of an explanation of another question, said something meaningful about her fears or hopes or about her travails dealing with the world. The existence of these fears is no surprise. Of course I deal with these issues, with and for patients, every day. What does come as a surprise is how much these comments color every aspect of how my patient and I interact.

Alida taught me this: the comments were always there. I had heard them before but had not given them the weight they deserve. I had not seen *myself* in these supposed *interactions*. I had underestimated patients' priorities. In the end, doing what I do, the priorities that I had set in ignorance may still be better responses to the patient's health needs than are her priorities, but, absent balance, dialogue fails.

Here are messages that patients give me—messages that I had to refocus in order to hear (the letters identify individual patients):

Message: I am never well (but, for the most part, I manage)

A. I never feel well, but for the last six months I haven't felt any worse than usual.

B. I manage. I'll do OK. It's not like it was before [when she was my patient; she now lives abroad].

C. I always feel like shit, but this is much worse than the usual shit. For the last two weeks I haven't been able to get out of bed, and I hurt everywhere.

D. I feel like shit, I always feel like shit. I'm exhausted. Everything hurts. You can't touch me anywhere. Even my [Caesarian section] scar hurts. Jesus! I'm only 38, not 78! I've got two kids to raise. I can't feel like this. Sometimes I want to give up. Or maybe I'm depressed. My father is senile. My brother-in-law is dying of AIDS. My mother is sick. My husband is trying, but he gets angry at me. I have to hide so much from him.

E. I haven't felt well for five years. None of those other things have worked. Why should this? Oh, I'm giving up. Do anything you want. You want to set it [an infusion] up? Do it. I don't care.

F. [woman who had just stopped her medicines in preparation to attempting pregnancy] Of course I hurt, but I don't want to do anything that will hurt my baby. It worked out the last time, didn't it?

Message: I am frightened about what the future will bring

G. I wake up most mornings wondering if it's going to come back. I worry that when I'm my mother's age I will be as sick as she is. [Speaker's mother has the same disease; speaker became ill at 15. Now 21, she has been in full remission for 5 years.]

H. [Card contains photograph of 19- and 15-year-old children of former patient, lethally ill when we first met, now living in the midwest] I'm so proud of the children…Dr. X [her new doctor] never really warmed up to me in four years, but he is very good and I am doing well…I'm divorced, but dating someone who doesn't seem to mind my history.

Message: I am optimistic (whether or not I have reason to be so)

I. *[The speaker's first pregnancy was nearly lethal; despite this she attempted a second pregnancy that was successful]* *We're trying again. How do you want me to manage my medicines?*

J. *Something wonderful has happened. I can go up stairs again. I almost feel normal.*

K. *(email)* *[Patient had just undergone an office procedure to complete a miscarriage.] Just wanted to let you know that I'm home. Everything went "fine." I'm a bit achy and crampy. On a brighter note...it was some of the best sleep I've had in about 2 months! Thanks again for all your support.*

Message: I am in conflict with my doctors or my family; I am not confident

L. *It's been a very rough couple of months [unrelated to arthritis.] Don't tell me anything I don't want to hear.*

M. *[a nurse, who is concerned that she cannot keep up with her job, accompanied by her son, who says] Tell her she is using too much pain medicine and that she shouldn't take so much.*

N. *[patient whom I had seen six years earlier for a second opinion, who had been advised to start aggressive therapy, returns for another second opinion] I just don't think it's right. I know my body. I don't think I need those medicines. [I agreed with her.]*

O. *[new patient with a probable diagnoses of both ovarian and breast cancer. I had just explained that the weakness and pain were almost certainly due to the tumors and would probably respond to their removal.] Oh, thank heavens. I've been telling my [other] doctors over and over that [the muscle weakness] had to be related and they just didn't agree and thought it was all in my head.*

Message: thank you for trying (even if things went wrong)

P. A gift, no comment, from a family of a long-time patient who died very suddenly two years earlier.

Q. A gift, no comment, from a husband of a severely ill patient who has undergone many surgical procedures and who, despite several attempts to detoxify, remains addicted to pain medications and who barely functions in society.

Next to my desk there is one of those little alarm/CD player/AM-FM radio sets that does everything nicely—a lazy man's entertainment center in seven inches cubed. Except: it is difficult to tune it to the right station. One turns a somewhat-hidden, ribbed, rotating wheel, gray on gray, somewhere on its right-hand side. The tuning knob is different from an identical but slightly-lower-placed volume control only because of an illegible embossed label, of the same color, that cannot be read unless one rotates the entire machine. I suppose the engineers had some important thought in mind, but it seems to me a terribly impractical design, and, failing to tune it properly, I often end up listening to salsa, not opera, even though the mood does not suit.

Talking to patients is a bit like tuning that set; it requires even more attention to be precise. If I turn the ribbed knob of our conversation just a tad more in this direction or that, I now know that I will hear a different tune. If the tuning is not precise, cacophony will ensue.

Or maybe, just maybe, I will be able to broaden my range and hear all the tunes.

I thought I had learned something important from my ability to hear. Patients' conversations do indeed contain leitmotifs. They put forth an unending theme that announces how chronic illness affects their lives.

I felt a little self-important when I made this "discovery." I shared the first draft of this chapter with Alida. I thought she would be impressed that I finally understood. She saw my discovery in an entirely different light. Her response was completely unexpected.

"I mean," she wrote to me by email, "honest to God, how DO you manage an entire population of us? I think perhaps another chapter here...not sure where it goes...but something about the "wear and tear" on physicians...I don't know... maybe it is a thing for the conversation. Each of us, in our own personal little canyon of misery and pain, but how often do we really think about what it is like to have a mountain of those sorts of messages and emails?"

I hadn't really thought about it being "a mountain of those sorts of messages." In fact, I hadn't really thought much about it at all. I shared the emails and my thoughts with my wife, who said, "Of course this affects you. Think of all those nights you haven't slept because you were worried about someone." True, but that isn't the point. To worry about one patient who is not doing well is a short-term event, not an accumulating mass of grief. It is a one-on-one, one-time thing: what is happening to this patient, what may I have missed, what decision might have been wrong, whether or not I should have done that test, whether or not I should have prescribed that drug.

These are concrete and time-limited concerns. I don't abstract from the personal to the larger scene and I almost never think that the disease is stronger than my tools, or that nature will win in the end. I think that the event will play out. There will be an end. We (the patient and I) will have won or lost. My concern will have applied to one person only and will not translate to the next patient I see.

The French poet and essayist, Paul Valéry, described a man he called Monsieur Teste, Mr. Head, the perfectly abstracted man, standing at the balcony rail of the Paris Opera, no personal self, just pure intellect, a mind studying and judging the crowd below.

I am not M. Teste. I am not on the balcony; I am in the crowd below. I am not standing apart, abstract, judgmental, on high.

I would, of course, be foolish to argue that physician burnout, high suicide rates, marital discord and other measures of stress do not exist. Numerous studies testify to the reality of the stress. To attribute them to an accumulation of patients' tales of misery, however, is wrong. I am not a psychiatrist and I do not wish to speculate on reasons how and why my colleagues respond as they do. Let me say instead that I do not believe the "mountain of those sorts of messages" is a credible cause of physician dismay.

I had not thought of the "mountain" before. That I had not surprises me. I *will* speculate on why I might have been so unaware.

I might have not seen the "mountain" because:

- It doesn't exist,

- It does exist, but I am blind to it,
- It does exist, I see it, but I am indifferent to it,
- It does exist, but it is counterbalanced by many good statements, or
- It does exist, but it is counterbalanced by other compensations in my life.

Regarding the first point, I don't think there is any question that the "mountain" exists. When Alida first spoke of the "mountain," I saw it instantly. Articulate something that should have been self-evident, it pops into view. It was everywhere I tuned my ear. The *leitmotif* of patients' conversations is very loud.

Regarding the second point, I certainly was aware. Some of the quotes from patients in the earlier chapters make it clear that, to a degree, I understood—I don't say incorporated into my soul—what they said. But Alida frames the issue as a global one (a characteristic of a class of patients rather than the concerns of individual patients) and so gives me an insight I had not had before—natural enough, since I do not think of myself as a prototype of a larger class. I think of the patient as "you" and myself as "me," just the two of us in a private struggle. For what I do, I think it may be better that way. A sociologist has a larger view.

Am I indifferent to the message? I don't think so, but it is not for me to judge. I worry about individuals, about relieving pain or preventing disability or protecting life—but I see these things from my vantage point, not Alida's, and not from that of the patient before me. That I feel wretched about a young girl's moon-shaped face or about a woman's inability to make long-term plans is different from seeing the misery through her eyes. As Alida says, I am a visitor to and not an inhabitant of her world.

A more cogent explanation of why the "mountain" does not weigh so heavily on me lies in the compensations I have in the office and at home. At the office—well, it is not a constant litany of woe. Interspersed among the bad are some thrilling, inspirational, and joy-giving tales. I see people who had once been extremely ill who are now doing quite well. In the same week in which I listened to the *leitmotifs,* I saw two young women whose lives had once been disrupted by strokes who had recovered and had moved on to exciting lives; a lady with a potentially lethal form of blood vessel inflammation who was able to plan a vacation for the first time in three years; several people in good remission; a few new consultation patients whom I reassured were not seriously ill; and a young woman with juvenile arthritis who, barely able to walk when I had first met her, had had her hips replaced, was walking beautifully, and now had a boyfriend and an engagement ring. These are moments enjoyed one by one that I can and do share. Mountain ranges can contain deeply lovely and verdant passes as well.

The good periods do not cause giddy ecstasy any more than the bad ones cause constant gloom. That a patient does well is an individual joy limited in time. This event will play out, and the remission may end, or the next person I see may be in the midst of a flare. Joys do not accumulate. Pleasure, as well as pain, occurs one at a time. I experience both in a world of you and me, doctor and patient. The experiences occur in the here and now, not as abstractions.

Home life is compensation as well. My wife will read this before you do, and I don't say these things very well. I get embarrassed when I say them, and so I will be brief: I am very fortunate in my personal life. My wife and daughter, (sometimes even the dog) are the best I could desire. I have had good luck as well: we all are in reasonably good health, have endured no major tragedies, and succumbed to no insurmountable money worries.

So there you have it. I did not see the mountain until Alida pointed it out. I don't know that my attitude would have changed had I been more aware. But, I am not Monsieur Teste. When I see patients I don't stand aside to watch myself to see how I do. True, I could be more analytical if I did abstract myself from the scene, but self-analysis is not my goal. It sounds quite narrow, I know—but a doctor, working with a patient, does act narrowly. We, the patient and I, start at point A and move to point B. From B we move to C, and thence to D. That seems to me to be sufficient for now.

MDL

Interdependence: The Doctor Moves to NIH

As patients can leave doctors or move away, doctors also have lives independent of their patients that are subject to change. At a mid-career point—some might call it mid-life crisis—I bought a sports car and decided to devote my career to medical research policy. I moved to Bethesda, Maryland, outside Washington, D.C., to work for the National Institutes of Health. I left Alida and my other patients behind, thinking to myself, pompously; I have a more important thing to do.

More important? Maybe, depending how you view the world. Later I would think, "Medical policy is an oxymoron." I should have known.

"Medical" is what doctors and patients do one-on-one, the battles with insurers, the negotiations about treatments, the short- and the long-term decisions, the shared joys and the shared pain. "Policy," especially national policy, decisions made for groups, and shared large-population goals, does affect what happens in the office and the bedside—but, to the young practicing doctor, meaning myself, the process by which national policy is made seems impossibly remote. How can those sitting around conference tables in black suits, staring at projected PowerPoint slides, debating clauses, know what is truly at stake?

Then the young doctor accepts assignment to a local committee, becomes a worker bee to do some unglamorous, onerous task to help solve a local need. Academic medicine breeds such committees. They proliferate at the speed of light.

Local committees send representatives to national committees. At some later point the doctor, who thinks he understands what happens in the office and the laboratory, the doctor whose first committee was very small and very local, finds himself on that national committee, then chairman of that committee, and then chairman of another. He discovers that, through these committees, he can *influence* the national rule—an ego-fulfilling thought, a possibility for doing greater good.

By chance (as he sees it; who knows what machinations were at play?) there comes a telephone call from a powerful man in Government, followed by a second, and a third, inviting him to apply for a second-in-command Federal job reporting to the caller, a job in which he can *create* policy and bring his one-on-one doctor-patient perspective to the national scene. From a family and personal standpoint the stars are in conjunction: it is a good time to make this move, and the doctor does. I did.

But what of the other family, the patients whose lives are intertwined with mine, from whom I would now take leave? For some of the patients the relationship was never more than a commercial transaction. Switching to another doctor for those people is a small matter. For other patients there were tears—on both sides—and an attempt to arrange ongoing care. And moments of anguish: some patients were very sick (Alida among them) and I did not want to leave them to another's care.

It was a huge source of frustration—actually, the word *frustration* is a gross understatement—for me to learn that many of my colleagues did not want to see my patients. Some had practices that were too full to expand. Other colleagues did not want the bother of taking responsibility for patients who were very sick. I begged some colleagues, cajoled others, threatened to refer patients to other hospitals and other universities, if I could not find someone to assume their care, until my supervisor intervened and commanded my colleagues to lend a hand. Still, I felt that I was abandoning my patients, who, I immodestly thought, depended on me. I tried to assuage my anxieties by telling myself that I was not so important, that there are many doctors more competent than I, and that no harm would come from the transition in care.

I later learned that my fears had in some cases been well founded and in other cases wrong. The switch to other doctors had helped some patients and had hurt others. One colleague changed my treatment plan for a very sick young lady and had effected an unanticipated cure. But another colleague dictated a fixed course of treatment for a patient who had a need to negotiate, and she withdrew from treatment and died.

I did go to Bethesda after all. There was a farewell party, and hugs and goodbyes and promises to stay in touch. For me, although the Federal facility is not structured for private practice, an arrangement was made whereby I was given permission to see patients one day a week, lest I forget my roots, a request that I had made as part of my contract to move.

Many of my former patients did stay in touch. Telephone calls and holiday greeting cards were routine. They sent pictures of children, of weddings, and of other happy occasions. Some made surprise visits and planned visits and lunch dates as they passed through town, and several came down just to have me check them out, reassure them that their new doctors were doing the right things. Sometimes long-term knowledge of patients helped. I saw a few things others had missed, or advised on options when routes were unclear. Sometimes just seeing a person doing well improved my day. Alida was among those who called and among those who came.

I did not lose the sense that I had abandoned those who were most desperately ill. In my practice life I had not run from the bedside of someone whom I could no longer save. Whether my staying with the dying is meaningful to the patient I cannot know, but it is important to me. If I am not there, if I am out of town, my sense that I have abandoned the patient is at its peak. Not long after I moved to Bethesda I had a terrible moment (as, of course, did the distraught teen-aged boy) when the son of one of my former patients called late at night and tearfully begged for some magic to save his mother, who was moribund and could no longer be saved. I had known that this day was going to come.

She did die. Many telephone calls and surrealistic days followed. The family asked me to sign my name to papers to affirm the good character of the deceased, so that proper papers could be filed in Pakistan, the country in which she had been born. I sought and found an Urdu translator and notary and signed my name to papers that I could not read and so, perhaps, had not abandoned her at the end.

Patients staying in touch created some startling moments. At one time I eagerly awaited the visit of a child, not seen for years, now sixteen years old, in my imagination all pink and frills and lace, whose mother's pregnancy had been deeply troubled and under my care—at last to greet a tattooed, pierced and studded apparition with sullen face and green spiked hair.

I had surprising deeply emotional moments, such as the time that, querying the source of a middle name, I discovered that a young lady in my "practice" in Bethesda was the grand-niece of one of my first, and most troubling, patients. Another time a handsome young woman sought me out at a public gathering to tell me she was the daughter of a patient of mine who had died shortly after her birth two decades before.

In the years I worked for Government I did not experience the emotional intensity that I had experienced when I was in practice, but I did, as I had wanted to do, devise national policy. I did play on the national scene. I did see ideas that had originated in my head slowly work their way up the bureaucratic chain to become national rules. The lag time between policy initiation and enactment is very long. Although I left Government more than a decade ago, I can still see some of the policy changes that I had proposed and initiated taking place today.

I also learned the politics of policy. I should have known, but did not at the time, that in policy decisions, when convictions are deeply held, truth does not matter unless it can be cogently sold. I repeatedly watched people present their cases truthfully but poorly and thereby lose arguments they should have easily won. I saw people who were untruthful and wrong speak fervently and compellingly and win, and I saw that, as a result of these false arguments, misdirected policy would ensue. During my stay in Bethesda Lyme disease, breast implants, fibromyalgia, and animal research advocates and detractors found themselves unable to negotiate positions civilly. The resulting policy was at times incoherent and often ignored.

I should have known more about the political world. It took me time to learn. Eventually I tired of the game. During my time in government I had not stopped thinking about the patients I had left behind. After a few years I began to obsess about how government policies affected these *individual* patients whom I had known. At night, at home, I began to write stories about them, placing my former patients into the context that the government rules, to which I now contributed, required. I saw my patients as individuals affected by and injured or advantaged by the rules made by strangers who knew neither their strengths nor whence they came. The stories became a book, the first non-medical writing I had ever done, that explored how federal rules touch each and every patient's life.

The more I wrote, the more vividly these people and these memories returned. One image brought forth another and still another. Whole conversations, smells, sounds, and emotions so raw they brought tears almost exploded in my mind in gaudy display. Living my life in flashback, I found people from my past virtually present in the room with me. Whether I was experiencing a flashback or hallucination, I saw that I had been very comfortable in the world of one-on-one medicine to which I belonged.

I was driving to Baltimore for another interminable policy meeting, the nature of which I no longer recall, when my cell phone rang. I answered, was put on hold for a minute, then was transferred to the husband of one of my former patients, a couple with whom I had stayed in touch. The husband was now a wealthy man. His wife was rapidly dying, he said. He wanted to make a gift in her honor that she could be told about before she died. The gift was to be a Center in her name, at the hospital in which she had been my patient, and where she was cared for now. The family had discussed this, he added. The purpose of the telephone call was to ask me to be the first director of that Center.

I would have to consider the offer for a few days, I replied (missing my exit on the freeway and causing me to be late for that meeting), to discuss it with my wife, and to think it through.

My reply had been dissimulation. I didn't have to discuss it further with my wife or to think it through one bit. She had already read what I had written, had seen the future, and was already enthusiastically urging me to move on. She is always right, and I did not disagree.

"Give me two days," I told the man on the telephone. It was not an "I should have known" situation. This was something I did know, deep in my heart, that I needed to do.

Two days later I returned the call and said, "Yes." A few months later I returned to the world of patients and friends.

MDL

When the Cat's Away...The Mice Will Play

Or, the patient will play doctor when the doctor is absent.

I did not see it coming. I am a social critic. I should have been more observant. Probably I noticed he was restless, but then so many of my friends were at the point at which you either make a career change or take a detour, or stay where you are for the rest of your life. When he told me that he had accepted a position at NIH, I projected my higher self in the face he saw in my response. I congratulated him and said it was important for someone like him to make public medical policy. My lower self, needy and scared, thought something else entirely. I felt abandoned, and I'm sure I certainly wasn't the only one.

I was in almost constant contact with him so I was fortunate to hear from him directly before he sent a formal letter to his patients. Knowing Michael, he probably told most of us in person or by telephone. I didn't know what to do, although there was a fleeting moment when I wondered if I could get a job somewhere in Washington and move. Then, of course, I realized that even if I wanted to uproot my Manhattan life, he was moving away from the private practice of medicine. Geography was less the issue than the form of medicine that would define him at NIH. I mentally ran through all the doctors that had been on-call for him, and was trying to figure out which one might understand my situation. One or two came to mind, but it didn't sit well with me. I made the presumptuous decision that I did not want to have a primary doctor inside the rheumatology service any more.

I expected to have quite a battle with Michael when I announced this, but surprisingly, he concurred. As my symptoms were mostly pulmonary at that point, we made a then-intelligent decision together. What I did not know was that Michael had not been having an easy time getting his colleagues to accept most of his most actively sick patients. They obviously had their own chronically ill patients. To add another group was not an easy sell.

I, however, felt I had outfoxed my doctor. I had triumphed over his departure, which I took personally, all the time celebrating his decision. I did come to see him at NIH, socially at first. He seemed happy enough there but, although he had been gone a very short time when I first visited he was not as I remembered him. It seemed as though I was seeing him through the other end of a telescope; though still warm and kind, he seemed distant and preoccupied. It was the bureaucratic setting, the corporate behemoth, that seemed strange to me. I had often been to NSF and to Census, and other such places, but they were filled with chatty social scientists. They were governmental agencies that took themselves far less seriously than did the one that makes decisions about our country's medical research policy.

While Michael was at NIH, strange things began to happen to me. I had new, weird symptoms. My back itched all the time. I had non-stop digestive problems. I lost weight. I thought it was stress or nerves or something connected to my disease. One day I looked in the mirror and my eyes were bulging. I called the doctor I had chosen as my primary physician and rushed to him. By then my heart was racing most of the time. I said something is really wrong with me. He was a chest doctor, so, of course, he listened to my lungs and said that I was fine. I said, "Do you think my eyes look funny?" He said that he didn't think so, that I always had large and beautiful eyes.

I left his office, having a sneaking feeling that he had missed something. I called my gynecologist and said I needed to see her for a minute or two. She invited me to come over, and so I did. I crossed into her office and she said, "My God, you have an extreme case of Graves' Disease." She wanted to know how long my eyes had bulged. I had no idea. She called a colleague of hers and I was on the way to his office within the hour. He took one look and pronounced me "toxic." (Funny. Because the technical name for the problem is thyrotoxicosis, the term probably meant something different to him.) He told me about Graves' Disease and ordered tests. He offered two options, one surgery and the other a "radioactive cocktail." He assured me that my eyes would return to my head and not be suspended in air for life.

I chose the cocktail. It did not make me glow in the dark, and it did arrest the Graves', but my eyes did not return to their normal place. I had waited too long. It was too late. The Mouse was not the Cat. I should not have been left in charge.

My Graves' Disease, although more or less dormant, has changed much about my life. Eyelid surgery followed and was not successful, nor were two additional attempts to cover my exposed eyeballs from sun and elements. Certainly, my eyes, always my favorite part of myself, have retracted some from the first days of my Popeye cartoon imitation, but they seem now someone else's, and always will be. When people compliment me about my large and lovely eyes, I can barely squeak out a polite word of gratitude. I take Synthroid® and will for life, not a big deal, many do. However, when a Wegener's lesion appeared in the socket of the left eye, it felt to me like the sucker punch and was followed by another hospitalization and immediate aggressive treatment.

During that emergency I was in California, but Michael

had returned to New York and had been running the Center for some period of time. This time my role as "doctor" worked out much better, since I was an advocate for myself and not a fake-physician. The California rheumatologist insisted that I needed immediate radiation to my eye. I called the ophthalmologist who had first discovered the lesion in my eye. She stabilized me with corticosteroid medication and shipped me back to New York and into Michael's care.

When I visited Michael at NIH after the first diagnosis of Graves' disease, I told him I had "blown it" and that I had really made a big error in choosing a doctor on my own. He said we had both been in error, and that the doctor he had left in charge of me had "dropped the ball." Well, of course he had. Even if his specialty was otherwise, he should have seen the symptoms as something, and called another doctor. But he did not. It wasn't out of incompetence or laziness or malice. He made an error. I had made an error. Michael had let me make a choice error because so few doctors wanted to deal with me and I had so liked the doctor who had helped save me from the worst of the spread of Wegener's years before.

Things happen in medicine with doctors and their patients. Doctors change careers or locations. Patients pretend they know more than they do. Doctors pay less attention than they should. Michael survived NIH. I survived Graves. We go forward.

Long ago I forgave the doctor who "dropped the ball." I didn't return to his care, but neither did I jump on the phone to hire a lawyer to sue for misdiagnosis or even contemplate doing so. He is a superb doctor of good will and brilliance in a discipline unrelated to what had happened to me. If there is any medical lesson to be learned from what happened to me during Michael's tenure at NIH, it is just how complex and trying it is to be in charge of chronically ill patients. It made me realize how overloaded the doctors' schedules are, how much anguish Michael must have felt upon hearing of the deaths of patients and all the avoidable and unavoidable episodes we, his patients, had to endure while he was stuck inside the vault of the exalted NIH.

While his departure is a blur to me because I blocked it out, his return was something else. That call was as unexpected as the one in which he said he was leaving. Suddenly, he was on the phone with the news that he was coming back, that a Center was being established for research about rheumatic disease and women. And, that he and his wife were looking at an apartment in my neighborhood and what could I tell them about the advantages of life where I lived.

From Graves' Disease and radioactive cocktails, sliced eyelids and too much eye makeup used as a disguise, the topic of our conversation fast-forwarded into a dizzy and happy discussion about the attributes of my neighborhood restaurants, the drug store, the dry cleaner, the deli, and all things Manhattan. Their return wasn't exactly like Fourth of July fireworks over the East River, but it came very close. Very close indeed.

AB

The Merchant of the Bronx

It is rare that I get an acute sense of nausea when I have seen a new patient.

To be sure, I have seen a host of unsettling but expected nausea-producing things: festering sores, profound problems of personal hygiene, violence, craziness, and lives unnecessarily destroyed by willful acts. That sort of thing is daily fare—well, maybe not daily, maybe bi-monthly or semi-annually—but I knew about that going into this business. I can't stop my body's reflexes from responding. In such cases, however, (I hope) I keep my cool, hide the internal emotions that see the societal injury that offends, the preventable part of the problem. It is the societal failure before my eyes, not the biological ugliness, that turns my stomach upside down.

Every so often I do exit an examining room truly appalled, and I ruminate on an issue for days. Whether I have dissimulated well, whether it is obvious to the patient how upset I am, I cannot know. It happens in circumstances and at times at which I am least prepared.

This past week I saw a new patient in what I thought would be a routine consultation visit. She was a young woman with failing kidneys who had come to our renal transplant service to prepare for a "pre-emptive" living-related donor transplant, pre-emptive in the sense that it would be done before dialysis was required. Something in her past had suggested that her blood contained an antibody that can cause the transplant to clot and fail. How to treat this antibody is more or less a specialty of mine. The transplant doctors and I have a plan for management of patients like her: I confirm the diagnosis and treat it before the surgeons do their thing. Routine stuff. Not highly challenging. Cut and dried. Rubber-stamped. Yes,

I concur. Initiate plan A.

The patient is an enthusiastic bundle of energy, a let's-get-this-moving-so-I-can-get-on-with-my-life type, going through her part of this necessary process as I was going through mine, both of us playing predictable roles without high interest on either participant's part. An attractive lady, girl to me, twenty-seven years old, articulate and well-informed, a salaried professional, almost annoyed to be losing time from work. She adored her doctors and was grateful because they had thought ahead and had suggested the pre-emptive transplant.

It is a little hard to describe this lady. New York is a multi-ethnic hub and she seems to be the very embodiment of this rich mix of language and cultures. Spanish name pronounced in the Anglo way, requisite tattoos, Bronx-accent, a New Yorker to the core. Regarding the tattoo: I never quite know what to do with the more flamboyant ones. I tend to comment, unnecessarily, on the strange Chinese or Sanskrit symbols or obscure insignias that are meaningless to me. But, this particular tattoo caught my eye: it was rather large, on the small of her back, and depicted a thin animal with pointed ears and a long curled tail, sitting on its haunches.

"Oh," I said, cheerily, and, of course, oblivious to its meaning. "What an interesting squirrel!"

It wasn't a squirrel.

It was meant to be a rather unpleasant cat, or maybe she said meerkat, I'm not sure. My impression of the tattoo didn't go down well; she had had a different image in mind. The conversation more or less deteriorated after that. I never found out what the significance of the animal might be, so I abandoned my foray into art criticism and returned to the matter at hand.

Her blood pressure was very high. "Oh," she said, in

sardonic imitation of my tone, when I mentioned the blood pressure. "It bounces all around. It is impossible to control." She was not concerned. In fact, her high blood pressure was why she first entered my medical world.

At age twenty-one she had felt a sudden numbness in her face and had been unable to move one arm. She had gone to a local emergency room in the Bronx. Her symptoms had improved over several hours. She was told her blood pressure was very high and that she had had a transient stroke. She was given medication, she said, and sent home.

Sent home! A twenty-one year-old with blood pressure so high that it had caused those symptoms—sent home! Then treated for high blood pressure for the next few years with no one asking why it was so high! I could not imagine how her doctors could have been so unconcerned. A couple of years later her kidneys began to fail—predictable, when blood pressure cannot be controlled.

She changed doctors. As far as I was able to piece the story together, her new doctor did an appropriate (but unreliable) blood test, found it negative and dismissed further thoughts on diagnosis. But he did do a kidney biopsy, a procedure the first doctor had thought too dangerous. The biopsy, she said, had been done about a year ago and was the reason she had been asked to consult me. The notes that had preceded her visit did not contain a copy of the biopsy report; apparently her doctor thought it gave evidence of the clotting disorder. At least it seems so, because he had prescribed anticoagulant medication after the biopsy had been done.

The medication did not help. Her kidney function got worse. Her doctor had referred her to our transplant team; because of what they had heard about the biopsy and the anticoagulation medication, they had referred her to me.

Now here is why my stomach turned: When I first saw her, before we had exchanged a word, I saw that their diagnosis was wrong, or at least that her doctors had missed something very important. From across the room, from fifteen feet away, I could detect that, from a certain pinching about her mouth, a smoothness of the skin of her face, the way she held her hands, indeed the very color of her hands, it was obvious that she had scleroderma, not the clotting disorder, or perhaps in addition to the clotting disorder. Knowing only that she had come for kidney transplant evaluation, I immediately guessed that she had scleroderma kidney disease, which begins with an abrupt and very severe blood pressure rise.

To be sure that I was not overstating the case, I asked to see her driver's license picture that had been taken a few years before—the cheapest of clinical tests. I looked at the license and then at her and back to each again. The disease had unmistakably been present when the picture was taken and it had progressed. There wasn't the slightest hint of a question about the diagnosis in my mind.

When I started my career most people with scleroderma kidney crisis died within a few months. In those days the only way to treat such patients was to remove their kidneys immediately, because the kidneys secrete a hormone that drives the blood pressure up to levels that kill. In the late 1970s—thirty years ago—I was privileged to witness the birth of a new class of drugs that completely block the kidney hormone and, for practical purposes, can cure scleroderma kidney disease, provided the diagnosis is made before the kidneys are permanently destroyed. In fact, I was the personal physician of the very last person in our hospital to have had her kidneys emergently removed.

Recognizing this diagnosis and treating it as an emergency

is one of the few things that rheumatologists do that can instantaneously save lives. Since the 1970s we emphasize and reemphasize the importance of the immediacy of this diagnosis—and its potential reversibility—to medical students and in-training doctors and doctors in practice. We keep a suitable drug easily available for emergency use. Suspecting the diagnosis, I have administered it in the office before sending a patient to the emergency room.

So, I had a completely different diagnosis, and a different plan for treatment, but she had other doctors, and she was said to have this antibody that causes clot. The support for that statement was the biopsy. The blood test that would confirm was not present in her chart. I had been told that the biopsy had shown that the antibody, not scleroderma, was the cause of her kidney disease. I did not have the biopsy report, let alone the actual slides. By nature, I like to dot my *i*'s and cross my *t*'s, so I called her other doctors then and there, each in turn, three in all, to get the report. None had the report available to fax to me.

Didn't have the biopsy report? Nausea increased. A young and energetic woman. An unusual circumstance, the blood pressure, the stroke, the kidney failure, all at an early age—and none of her doctors had (apparently) taken the extra step to find out why or to confirm a diagnosis and then check again? Who, I thought, just shrugs off a twenty-one year-old with a stroke? Who thinks, just another hypertensive? Just another anxious kid?

I said the lady was energetic. When I told her I was thinking of a different diagnosis and needed to see the biopsy, she offered to go personally to the hospital where the biopsy had been done to bring the slides to me—which she did at the beginning of the following week. I have a microscope in my examining room and I was able to look at the slides within the hour: scleroderma kidney disease to my eye, no clotting disorder at all.

A written report accompanied the slides. The report described the findings but mistakenly attributed the changes to a different diagnosis that was inconceivable in someone this young. The reading was wrong, but the person who had done the biopsy had given the pathologist no helpful information, not even her age, just a name and chart number, a compounding error, a casualness with her well-being, that for practical purposes guaranteed that the pathologist could not do his job.

I am not a pathologist, and I am not all that confident of my skills at reading kidney biopsy slides. It was after hours, so I emailed our head of kidney pathology, who invited me to bring the slides to her the following day. We read the slides together; the pathologist agreed they showed scleroderma, not the clotting disorder. Then she remarked, by way of curiosity, "I thought you said the biopsy was old, but this was done last week."

"No, I replied, "The patient said it was done last year."

"But look," the pathologist said, "it was read just five days ago."

And so it was stated, right at the top of the page, both the biopsy date and the reading date, incidental information that I had ignored. The biopsy had been done when I thought it had been, but the reading date was the day after I saw the patient, the day after I had called her doctors in alarm. No wonder her doctors did not have the report in their charts: the biopsy had not been read in more than a year—and, apparently, no one had called to ask for the report or to find out why!

The pathologist and I were both speechless, and could only

just stare at each other, dumbfounded at such negligence.

It was all there in black and white. This pretty, articulate, informed, energetic young woman had been failed by doctors in ways too numerous to count. Ever since the time she had first gone to the emergency room and for a year or two after, she has unknowingly been walking around with a reversible kidney disease, though now it probably is too late. It is more than likely, that, had someone paid attention back then, she would not need a transplant at all.

I wasn't there, of course. I don't know what the other doctors saw or what decisions they did or did not make. Perhaps they were overwhelmed with patients and did not have time to sit down and think. Perhaps the signs of scleroderma were too subtle for non-specialists to see. She is from the Bronx, where things are a bit different. The ERs are busier than in Manhattan, more crowded with violence and problems that occur with illegal drugs. Maybe it was a volume-of-patients thing, too much to do.

But then there is the other thing. I am not a cynic and I am not (very) judgmental, but as I sit here this evening turning this obsessively over and over in my mind, I find myself hoping—I really, really hope—that those doctors did not see just an energetic, talkative (would they have thought sassy? smart aleck?) Puerto Rican kid with a tattoo, someone dispensable. Then by association, *The Merchant of Venice* popped into my mind, Shylock without guile, or maybe Portia: Hath not a Puerto Rican eyes? If you prick them, do not Puerto Ricans bleed?

Or maybe it is a failure to understand that there is no forest absent the strength and individuality of single trees, that the person before you constitutes one of the elements within, but is not herself the crowd. This is a failure to understand, in other words, the very purpose behind what we doctors do. There are no crowds in medicine, there are only individual patients. Abstraction has its own role—big policy decisions flow from that—but patient care is always one-on-one, with full attention to the one.

The pathologist and I read the biopsy a few hours ago. I have not yet called the young lady to tell her my conclusion and that I want to make one last try to save her kidneys. I know it is probably too late, but maybe there is something still to save. Certainly I now know why her blood pressure is so high and I know how to get it down. That's the easy part.

The hard part, the reason I'm writing this tonight, rather than calling her right now, is that I just don't know what I can say.

I called the patient the next day, and she was surprised. It bothered her that I told her that she did not have the clotting disorder she thought she had. I told her to stop the anticoagulant medication. I also talked again to her other doctors. They changed her blood pressure medications in the way that I thought they should. She made appointments to do the necessary follow-up tests. The first one showed much more severe heart disease than I had assumed she had.

After that test she did not come back. She disappeared from view, and I heard nothing more. My calls were not returned, not from her, not from her other doctors. I was third in line in the consultation list, after her primary doctor and the transplant team, and their decisions have priority over mine. I cannot command her obedience to my whim, or theirs.

My guess is that one of the following may have occurred: either she or the other doctors disagreed and sent her elsewhere for another consultation; or she may have become very depressed and may have withdrawn from the transplant plan entirely; or she may have been told that she was no longer eligible for transplant (not true in my estimation); or perhaps her insurer, which covered the transplant team but not me as "preferred provider," may have forbidden further investigation on my part; she may have responded to unpleasant news by pretending that it is not true—closed her eyes to the shadow, focused only on the dream; she may have become too ill, though I doubt this, because I probably would have heard.

I have been in this place before and I know what will happen. Sometime in the future she will return, or one of her physicians will tell me what transpired. I can be patient. I have to be. When doctors have different opinions, or when patients disagree with my opinions, the patient's desire prevails. Eventually I will know. For the present, however, I still do not sleep because I believe that a treatable young woman has missed a chance for better health. I do not sleep because, not having gained her confidence, or not having gained the confidence of her referring physicians, I have failed her too.

Two months later she did come back.

She used information as her talisman. She sought information on the Internet and in other places that she did not share with me but that I can surmise. She needed time and facts to adjust to a new diagnosis and a new plan.

When she came back she was not confident. She looked thin and a tiny bit scared. She asked what was going to happen to her. She talked about her transplant not as when but if—because, with what she had learned, she now understood she might not live to see the transplant occur. Now I was the optimist, telling her that we can get through this together if we both work hard—a switch of roles.

To work out the new relationship between us took a few more weeks. Now she returns my calls and comes in to be seen. (Not easy: her insurance does not cover her visits [I do not charge], and she loses time from work.) Then her original personality began to re-emerge. She joined a scleroderma group. She volunteered for a walk-run fund-raiser for this disease. She was back, taking charge again.

Today her blood pressure is under much better control. She monitors it at home; she sends me emails to report. We both know that her kidneys are going to fail. So be it. We can move to transplant much more safely than we could before. The first—my early—goal was to secure her life. We accomplished that goal, or at least we made a good start. The rest is mere comment.

I sleep again, but I dislike that I pulled rank, threatened a patient with dark prognostic facts, deliberately destroyed her confidence, in order to get to the place we both needed to be.

I dislike knowing that we engaged in a test of wills which I may or may not win but which she can only lose. I dislike knowing that I took advantage of my position vis-à-vis hers, professional vs. lay, Manhattan vs. Bronx, male vs. female, senior vs. young, white vs. brown, and had asserted control.

I made her distraught for what I had perceived to be her good. I justified that arrogance by my belief that her vision did not see beyond the *uinal* and the *tun* while my vision was of the *katun*, the thirty-seven or forty-seven or even fifty-seven-year-old in my mind's eye that in her youth she cannot yet foresee but that I hope she will one day become.

Powerful thing this, the training and license that grant me the ability to destroy or sustain another's dream.

Sobering and frightening and nauseating thing this, the

knowledge that I sometimes actually do exercise this power.

Humbling thing this, to be able to use this power, once in a while, to salvage lethal mistakes, made seriatim, on a cheeky Puerto Rican kid with a tattoo.

MDL

Things Go Wrong: A Patient Named Carole

I have never taken the exact tally of the times I have sat at the deathbeds of good friends, present with them until the very end. If I did, it might depress me. It is probably a larger number than the national average for people my age not in the medical profession. Interestingly, it is not because I have made close friends with other patients suffering from diseases similar to mine. Mostly, they have either died from cancer or were victims of unforeseen and horrible accidents.

It isn't that I embrace death or look forward to its arrival, but I suppose I've stared it down and therefore I won't stand aside for it and allow it to keep me from being the friend I want to be to my friends as they leave. It is certainly the case that nothing about what happens at the end scares me or makes me squeamish. I never think about it. What I think about is how lonely the tunnel must be as you begin to enter it and know, with whatever is left of your reasoning power, that you can't back out of it.

I spoke of death as the tunnel when I wrote about the loss of my friend in an earlier book. Her death remains of consequence to me for reasons both profoundly personal and professional. And, then there are those other losses that I can't write about because they would bring me too much pain to recall. There are other deaths I choose not to write about because of what the person's death did to me, or because writing about my involvement would violate the privacy of others, or because the loss is still too fresh.

There is one death, however, that I have never spoken about, but the memory of which now and then returns, at times when I least expect it.

It is not a long story, but it is one that I must no longer

keep silent.

At a hospital, many years ago, in a four-bed "ward," I became friendly with the woman directly in the bed across from me. She was probably in her early forties. It was hard to tell how old she was because her face and body were so disfigured by disease and drugs. She was an uneducated, unpleasant, angry and frightened working class white woman. She was very sick with a form of lupus that had gone undetected or wrongly diagnosed until, well, until it was far too late.

She had a large and loving family, somewhat crude in their manners and absolutely lost without any guide or maps to the medical world in which they found themselves. Someone from her family, or some subset of them, tried to be in the room when the rounds of doctors would come to see us. After they left, one of the family members invariably would come over to me, call me "the professor,"—because I worked at a university research center—and ask me if I had any idea what the doctors had told them.

I was so worried that they were without adequate protection of the information needed to make informed choices about what should happen, that I asked a nurse if she could get a patient's advocate for my ward-mate. She said it wasn't my business. She was right, it wasn't. I didn't press it.

The woman's name was Carol—but, I think, with an "e" at the end—Carole. She was hopelessly ill. I could see that. Yet, somehow, her family couldn't see it. Her father came and sat by my bed one night and told me that he had taken her to many doctors from the time she was in her late teens. If she were then about forty, he must have been about seventy or even younger. Whatever his chronological age, he seemed very old, and defeated. Everything he believed in as an American, and a patriotic one, had failed him. His union had failed him. His medical plan had failed him when she was still young enough to be covered by his insurance. Her employer had failed her. Our national ideology of equality for all was a joke for her and her entire family.

I want to believe that the world that Thomas Jefferson and John and Abigail Adams, my favorite founders, envisioned for all of us is more of a reality today than it was in that hospital ward, but I do not think much has changed. We remain, despite all of our protestations and all of the political jargon flying across both sides of the aisle, a profoundly elitist country when it comes to who gets what kind of health care and intervention, and who doesn't.

Carole should never have been allowed to be reduced to the miserable heap of suffering I witnessed day in and day out. Somebody should have answered her relentless screams of fear and pain during the night, but no one did. Most nights, I would get up out of bed, I.V. stand and all, and sit with her. Another woman, in the bed next to her, old and frail, would relieve me at some point in the night, and we would touch each other but not speak. She was a retired elementary school teacher; she could add two plus two just as well as I could.

Carole began to run a high fever one night and, by having my own spectacular, eloquent tantrum, I got the nurses and then lots of doctors into the room. She was soaking wet, delirious, and probably in wrenching pain. A doctor, who was the resident on call, said that they had to perform a surgical procedure of some type right then, and they asked her to sign a consent form. I began to protest to all of them, that someone should call her family first before she signed the form. The nurses, and other attending medical staff, snapped closed the curtains around my bed. I shut up, and wept.

I thought to myself that, by insisting that the doctors

attend to her, I had undoubtedly just brought down the curtain on her life. It was too late. I had done what I thought I should have done, but I have never been at peace with the decision I made when I went tearing down the hallway in righteous indignation over what was happening.

The morning finally dawned, and there was no Carole in the bed across from me. She never came back to her bed. She died during the surgery. Her parents came to get her things. They were silent as they gathered up her few articles of clothing and magazines. They wanted to thank the older retired schoolteacher and me for all we had done. I hugged them both, and they said, "Jesus has her now, so it's fine."

The teacher asked me if I thought it was fine after they had left. I said I thought Jesus was quite irrelevant in this case; that I thought it was malpractice that had taken her away and not Jesus. She said she thought so too. She said how glad she was that she was educated, and that I must be very grateful for that too. I asked her if she thought Carole ever understood a thing that the doctors said to her. She said she was sure that she did not, and that neither did her family. I agreed.

I called a close friend and asked him to come and get me. He was surprised, thinking that I had been discharged early. I told him I had not been discharged. It was the weekend, and I was checking myself out of the hospital. He tried to reason with me. I said he could come or not, but if he didn't come, I was likely to walk all the way back to my home from the ward by myself. He said I was being ridiculous; I should wait until Monday and learn what my latest tests indicated. He felt I had developed the hospital version of cabin fever; he would bring me some lunch. He would stay and visit with me and I would feel better.

I said he should listen to what had happened to Carole,

my roomie, as he liked to call her. As he would enter our ward, he always called out, "and how's my favorite roomie?" She was unaware that he was one of the most distinguished scholars in the country. He would never have let her know that. Although a hyper-intellectual all the way, this friend of mine had developed a true tenderness for her. He had studied populations of poverty-stricken people in the developing world, and in the United States. He understood things about her I didn't. We understood Carole's situation and circumstances well, but from different perspectives.

My friend did come to get me. I signed myself "out against doctor's orders" on the forms. Or, released without medical consent is what one of the "Carole-killers" said to me in a snotty voice. I started to say he had killed my roommate, but my friend shut me up quickly. I was a raving radical revolutionary all the way home. I told him I was going to quit doing research and start a national patients' rights advocacy organization. He told me I needed to finish my own work, which he insisted in his quiet but firm way, was more important. I was angry and argued with him to the extent of my ability, in the grip of exhaustion and illness. He stocked my house with food and arranged with other friends to run relays to look in on me, until they could decide what the hell to do with me, their friend, colleague, and runaway patient-revolutionary.

Then, he said these words to me:

"Alida, don't stop doing your research. Just write about this someday. Write about the inequality that uneducated people face in our system. Write about it as one of the greatest immoralities of our society. Write it out in order to right the wrongs."

I finally have.

I only wish he were still alive to read these words. I let

Carole down that night, but maybe I haven't let my friend down, in the end.

Unfortunately, our system still fails the "Merchants of the Bronx" and the "Caroles" each and every day. There is more to health care reform than simply providing insurance for everyone. We must somehow find a way to provide an equality of understanding for all, regardless of economic status or level of education.

AB

A Doctors' Life: Phase 1 Trials

Not all patients get better. Not all treatments work. Some patients do not tolerate the side effects of certain drugs; others do. Miracle cures are everywhere. New medicines are in the news every day, on television and on the Internet. Patients ask me to try something new. Alida has asked me to try something new. "Why can't I," the patient asks, "get access to this cure?"

"Because," I say, "I can't prescribe it. It is available only in a clinical trial. Yes, we are (sometimes) part of this trial. You may be a candidate for the trial—let's see."

So what about these trials?

Can, and should, my patients be guinea pigs? When a new drug is being tested to treat her disease, should I push her forward or tell her to stay away? Let's not fantasize about informed consent and free choice here. Every doctor knows that the way he presents an option, the way in which he or she says, "If you were my (wife, parent, sibling, child), here is what I'd do," determines the patient's response nine times in ten.

Hypothetically, if I want a patient to join a trial, I can put on my authoritative face, stress the upside, pooh-pooh the downside, and it is done. If I want the opposite response, a simple, "Your choice, but if I were you I wouldn't," says it all. It is not that patients are so pliable. It is that I, having more information, unconsciously or deliberately, can present the story whichever way I choose.

I wish discussing a clinical trial were that easy.

Let's put a few facts on the table. I've been in practice over thirty-five years. When I started, we treated rheumatoid arthritis patients with aspirin, gold, and prednisone, and most patients ended their shortened lives in wheelchairs. Now we have new, really terrific, medicines, and most patients continue with fully functional lives. Crippling is now uncommon, and life has been prolonged. Another example: deaths were an everyday event for doctors treating lupus patients back then; pregnancies were out of the question. Lupus was an absolute indication for elective abortion before *Roe v. Wade.* Now lupus deaths are rare, pregnancies common, and most of the management issues focus on drug side effects and prevention of complications.

We didn't get from then to now without some patients offering their bodies for the testing of unknown drugs, possibly trading their well-being for a future good. Of course, consent forms are far more formal these days—the doctor's obligation to provide information is a good deal more regulated now than it was then. Consent forms often are twenty pages or more, single-spaced, in (allegedly) eighth-grade language, detailing all the bad and little of the good. Not that these consent forms are all that helpful. Most patients choosing to join a trial, look at the forms, toss them aside, and simply ask, "Where do I sign?"

Recruiting a patient to join a trial isn't a matter of my choosing or not to ask. Each trial has its own particular constraints that worry me. Each patient has her own that worry her.

The first question I ask myself (before I do or do not choose to recruit) is: Is this a phase I, phase II, phase III, or phase IV trial?

A phase I trial tests toxicity and dose, nothing more. It is small-scale, involving only a few persons who may be normal or who may be ill with a specific disease. The drug will have been given to mice and monkeys; it appears to be safe. A phase I trial asks this question: What happens when we give this drug to a human? When we give it at one-tenth or ten times the predicted dose? In a phase I trial it is nice if something good happens to the patient, but a good response is not the point. Toxicity is. That's what a participant in a phase I study does—proves that the drug is or is not too dangerous to begin a trial. The participant usually has no option to get the drug after the trial is done. At best, if the drug moves forward, she may be first in line to receive it once it is approved.

Because of the animal tests and pharmacological science, the risk to the patient is generally not high, but, in the Spring of 2006, in England, four of six healthy volunteers, each having been paid £150 to test increasing doses of a new product, rapidly became critically ill and ended up in intensive care wards. All survived, but their recoveries took weeks. Careful analysis after the fact found a few minor hints that might have suggested what was about to occur—little stuff, an *i* undotted here, a *t* not crossed there, but nothing that really stood out. The biggest problem was that four were affected rather than one, because the company hadn't waited as long as it should have done between subjects, verifying that subject 3, for instance, was fully well before going on to subject 4. Had they done so, there would have been only one or two, not four, who fell ill. But that person would still have fallen ill. This is the non-predictable part of doing trials.

In the most cynical sense, a chance to participate in a phase I study is a chance to be harmed—with no possibility of personal gain. Why would I ever recruit a patient for a phase I study? Generally I do not, while other more enthusiastic colleagues do, but sometimes, just sometimes, my close colleagues are working on the theory behind this drug and need to know more. In that case I may introduce the patient to the investigator but my involvement stops there, I neither advocate nor dissuade, and I do not know whether I have done right or wrong.

A phase II study is an efficacy and dose-ranging study: the drug has passed its toxicity screen. Does it do (in the very short term) what it is expected to do? At what dose? A phase II study is small, usually involving groups of ten or twenty patients. Usually, because of the short time for doing tests to approve the drug, a phase II trial succeeds or fails if blood tests improve rather than the patient gets better. After all, you can't test a drug for ten years. As with a phase I trial, the patient has no option to continue the treatment for many reasons: There is not enough drug available, its long-term effects are unknown, safe dosing is not known, and the Food and Drug Administration (FDA) does not permit its further use. A person participating in a phase II trial may be the first to experience a good effect but may have to wait for further proof from tests in other patients before she can get long-term access to the drug. Of course, if the drug cures her very quickly, that is fairly dramatic, but such good luck rarely occurs.

Phase III trials test drugs against standard treatments or against placebo, usually in several doses. The question Phase III asks is: Is this drug good enough to bring to market? A phase III trial patient may or may not receive the drug, will usually continue on standard therapy, and, if receiving drug and not placebo, will be among the first either to benefit or to be harmed.

The potential benefit for the patient is greater in a phase III than in a phase I or II trial and the risk is less because of the information obtained in the earlier trials. The benefit to the patient is a chance to get the new drug; the downside is that the patient may be in the placebo arm and may miss out on something good. Of course, phase III studies sometimes bring out unanticipated toxicities that were not seen with smaller studies. Drugs that successfully pass phase III can be presented to the FDA for approval for sale.

Phase IV studies are post-marketing studies. The drug has been licensed and is now prescribed and sold. The earlier studies tested it in at most a few thousand people. Drug companies are required by law to see what happens when a new drug is used by hundreds of thousands, looking for rare side effects not seen in smaller trials. Vioxx® was pulled from the market because phase IV studies showed that it caused too many heart attacks; other drugs have similarly been withdrawn.

So my first question is about the study itself: what phase is the study? The next questions are about the patient: does she need to change course in the treatment of her disease? What are her other options? Phase I studies usually recruit patients who are stable or for whom nothing else can be done, a pretty limited group. For the other phases, either the patient or I can suggest that it is time for a change. There is no point recruiting stable patients who are doing well. For this patient, though, it may be that we have run through everything possible. It may be that she hates the side effects of the medications she is now taking. It may be that she is altruistic or adventuresome. It may be that a news story or a web statement or something else promised an immediate cure. Sometimes it will be that I have heard about this product, believe that it is theoretically sound, have some information of its safety and think that it will be very hot, that it will dramatically change the treatment we have today. There are many reasons for either the patient or me to consider a phase II or III trial.

My final question is to the patient: what would you like to do? This is full disclosure time (to the patient; to you, the reader). I coordinate some clinical trials at our institution. My friends have developed some of the products we test. (I have no financial relationships with any of the companies involved.) I take care of many patients who are potential candidates for these trials. I also sit on administrative boards that oversee clinical trials.

If I recruit a patient, I know that by pitching the story a certain way, I can influence whether or not he or she joins a trial. So I have established a personal rule: I explain that the trial is underway, but someone else, a colleague or a study coordinator, will talk to the patient about the trial. During the recruitment period—I tell this to the patient—I will not advise for or against her joining the trial. My stance, regardless of which phase, is that if I am your doctor, I am your advocate. I don't want to confuse the roles.

Does this sound simple? It really is not. At this moment I am advising a young doctor. In college, and her first year in medical school she was desperately ill; then she recovered brilliantly. She completed school on time, graduated, took a residency, and became engaged. Recently she developed a disease complication that is rare and that doesn't fit the usual rules of her disease. Consultant specialists in the complication (the blood pressure in the artery leading to her lungs suddenly became very high) joined the team, and right now the consultants and I have modestly divergent views about what to do.

The consultants are convinced that her basic illness (about which I have considerably more experience than they do) is driving what has now gone wrong. The consultants are calling for much more aggressive treatment (a chemotherapy drug called cyclophosphamide) than the lower potency but less toxic drug that she now takes. They are also asking for a major surgical procedure, a lung biopsy, to prove that they are correct. I am not convinced, but I can offer no better explanation or plan. Cyclophosphamide is quite miserable for a young woman; she will lose her hair and will likely become sterile if she takes it. She will likely lose her job and her fiancé also. And, I don't even know whether the drug will work.

I am the principal investigator at our hospital for a phase II clinical trial that she could join. In this trial two of every three patients will receive a new drug. The drug has been widely used in other circumstances but not in her disease. It is quite easy to take. So far as we know, and we know a lot, its side effects are not dangerous and not unpleasant. The new drug is very expensive. I can prescribe it outside the trial, but she can't afford it and her insurance will not pay. If she receives the drug in the trial and gets better we likely can convince her insurer (or the company that is sponsoring the trial) to supply it again. If she is in the placebo arm, she will be eligible to receive the drug when the study is done, but that will take a year.

So, I don't know that the drug will work—it is experimental because it has not been used in her disease—she has a 33% chance of not receiving it, and, if the consultants are right and I am wrong, she should be treated with the very unpleasant drug. However, it is also true that because the blood pressure problem in the lungs is so rare, we don't actually know that cyclophosphamide will work; we know about the benefit of cyclophosphamide because it works in a different aspect of the disease. It may not work for this problem at all. If the consultants are wrong and I am right, we don't need to do more than we currently are.

She and I have been negotiating this issue for the past week or two. We communicate often by emails. This is what she wrote last week:

> *After a week of thinking about the options you presented to me,*
> *I have a few questions for you:*
>
> 1. *Will the results of a lung biopsy change treatment decisions?*
> 2. *If I join the [experimental drug] trial, there's no guarantee*
>   *that I'll actually get the drug, right? Isn't it a double-blinded,*
>   *randomized trial?*
> 3. *I am feeling better than a month ago. There is some improvement,*
>   *but I don't know if I should be expecting faster improvement.*

By habit, I answer complicated emails like this by typing my responses in capital letters following the question. Here's what I replied:

1. *IF IT DOES SHOW VASCULITIS THAT*
   WILL BE UNEQUIVOCAL REASON
   TO TREAT VIGOROUSLY.

2. *THE OPTIONS ARE (1) CONTINUING THE*
   DRUG AND RECEIVING PLACEBO AND
   (2) RECEIVING [the experimental drug] AND
   CONTINUING THE DRUG YOU ARE ON.

3. *I DON'T KNOW HOW FAST YOU*
   SHOULD EXPECT TO IMPROVE.

4. *I'M THINKING THAT I WOULD LIKE TO*
   BE MORE AGGRESSIVE THAN [the drug
   you are on]—NOT CONVINCED THAT'S
   NECESSARY, BUT LEANING THAT WAY—

*SO I THINK THE [experimental drug] IS THE
INTERMEDIATE OPTION (ASSUMING YOU
QUALIFY), AND I'M SAYING THAT NOT
BECAUSE I AM PART OF THE STUDY BUT
BECAUSE I'M PUSHING FOR THE BEST
OUTCOME WITH THE LEAST TOXICITY.*

There you have the dilemma of clinical trials. I believe in the new drug but I don't actually know that it will work. I believe it is safe, but, in my role as a monitor of another study, I have seen people with this young lady's illness (but different manifestations) get into serious trouble, possibly as a result of the drug.

As her physician, I want to do what is best, easiest, and least toxic for her. As principal investigator of the trial in question I feel deeply conflicted about recruiting her directly—it can always be said that I just wanted to increase the numbers in the trial and did not have her welfare in mind. I don't believe that is true, but if I recruit her I will not be able to refute the assertion. If I do recruit her, and if she receives the placebo and gets worse, my guilt will be enormous. If I recruit her and she receives the drug and markedly improves I will not feel much better because I know in my own mind the chances that we took. Beyond that, she is the most informed of patients. I have known her and her family for years. She looks to me for advice, as she should.

There you have it. I hate recruiting for clinical trials. I hate the conflict of interest. I despise asking someone for whom I am responsible to take a chance with her own health for me.

Had this young doctor fallen ill when I started practice, she would have been two decades dead. Back then, other doctors had recruited patients for other trials. Because of the volunteers who preceded her, and because of the doctors who recruited those volunteers, she is now here, able to ask me what she should do.

What we do today may shift the paradigm for tomorrow. It is possible that my offer to this lady will be the first (or fourth or 10th or final) step forward in the development of a future cure. Or not. It may fail. It may harm her as well.

And there is an irony: if we make the wrong choice we will probably know soon. Disasters tend to occur in a visible time frame. If we make the right choice, response in chronic disease tends to be slow. We will not likely know we were right for years.

Do I prioritize the individual or the common good? Does she go with the tried and true (actually, in this case, not so tried and not so certainly true), or does she take a chance?

There is no right answer to these questions and no peace of mind. She and I, we share the facts, we negotiate, and together we decide. I can't and won't oversell this trial. Perhaps I do her a disservice if I undersell. So I put the decision to her. She will talk to my colleagues. I will not advise.

I pray that her decision will be, and that mine was, a wise one.

MDL

A Summer Wedding

On a cloudless summer afternoon, on the grass courtyard of an open-air chapel, at 6:00 in the evening, in the presence of a modest number of friends and family, the young doctor said, "I do."

Actually, she and the groom said, "I will," because the minister had said, "Will you take..." or "Wilt thou take..." I am not sure: the voices did not carry very well. The rest of the vow followed the familiar words. "In sickness and in health" remained. The groom is also a doctor—they first met in medical school. He knows that this is not a casual vow. He said his words loudly and clearly and looked directly into her eyes. He did not hesitate. His voice did not break. As best I can tell, my heart was the only one that stopped, and mine the only breath that held, as he said those words. But, of course, their backs were to me, so I could not read the bride's or her mother's eyes.

Good-looking even on an average workday, on this day the bride was breathtakingly beautiful. Years earlier the bride's skin had been marked by the kind of rash that makes people shy away, but today it was flawless from her scalp to the top of her strapless bridal gown. Her hair, once thinned by illness, was long and full and swept upward in a fashionable chignon.

All the older relatives had been born in lands far away. My wife and I stood out, so at the reception questions were asked. I said that I was her professor from medical school, an answer that appeared to satisfy most. I am often reticent at such happy occasions. I worried that my presence will bring back memories of the bad times and spoil the mood of the day. I need not have feared. At the reception, when we congratulated the couple and their immediate kin, the hugs were tight and prolonged.

The bride did not participate in the clinical trial. I had prescribed the less toxic of the conventional drugs. She did not do the lung biopsy. We had walked—together—a middle ground. We had gambled among options when the way was not clear. For the time being we had won. Her health continued to improve, as she had insisted that it would.

At the reception, my wife and I watched this young bride, who a year earlier could not have crossed a small room without gasping for breath, dance and dance, first the vigorous dances of her American generation and then the exotic ones of her ancestral land, then run across the room to give us a final hug as we, exhausted by her energy and the late hour, rose to leave. The sun had long gone down. The dream of her recovery suffused the atmosphere of this ballroom on this cloudless, beautiful summer night, and, one hopes, will continue to do so for a very long time to come.

MDL

A Doctor's Life: Annie, or It's In My Bones

Alida makes it very clear that patients do not always like their doctors. The reverse is also true. I would like to think that I am discrete about such matters but, like it or not, some stories do come home with me. We all need to decompress some times. Tales do get told at home.

When I first met Annie, she was extremely shy, pathologically timid, easily terrified. A sudden movement, a loud noise, an unanticipated event would make her tremble and sometimes run and hide. Even before I met her I knew about her fears. She had been described to me before I opened the door.

Annie in her early life had been physically abused, I had been told. She had been taken from her home, given medical treatment, and placed in foster care. Now, years later, she was physically strong but emotionally still in need of considerable care. In the five years since Annie has matured, she is assertive, confident, even imperious at times. My wife and I speak with irony about the change. Annie is "self-actualized," we say. She lives in instant time.

My wife told me I was to blame. After all, Annie is our daughter's rescue dog. Our spoiling, and my feeding her at the table, made her this way. This conversation had begun because Annie had (rather rudely) inserted herself into our conversation at late lunch—a lunch that took place hours after it was due, by her reckoning. As was her wont, she was making little 'hrrrmpph'ing sounds in case I missed the point. With one quick upward jerk of her powerful nose she nudged my arm (translation: my arm flew skyward, the contents of my fork widely dispersed) to remind me to give her a piece of chicken. She knew that I would. I did. I fed her at the table, as I, to our daughter the disciplinarian's disgust, always do.

After the meal Annie, as she always does, ran to the cabinet in which her treats, Greenies—doggie cocaine—are stored, and there she stamped her feet and in a saccadic rhythm pointed with her head and hrrrmpph'ed again until we produced her dessert. Self-actualized, indeed. No deferred gratification here. Instant time. "You brought it on," my wife said. "You taught her to do this." And I confessed, "I couldn't help it. It's in my bones."

The comments on Annie's upbringing and transformation logically followed what we had been discussing before. An emergency page had delayed our Saturday lunch. A not very ill patient, a young mother, whom I had known for years but had not seen for many months, had ignored the "for emergencies only" statement on my recorded telephone message, had asked the service to page me instantly, in order that I call in a prescription for an over-the-counter analgesic, naproxen, that she sometimes took.

She could have left a non-urgent message, she could have called on Friday or Monday, she could have gone to the drugstore or corner store or grocery and bought it on her own—it is inexpensive, and she is not poor. But her thinking was that she wanted it now and the purchase would cost her less if prescribed and bought through her health care plan. That I actually did call in the prescription is unimportant. My staff calls in many such prescriptions every office day. But being paged on a Saturday afternoon to do emergently what could easily be done in a normal office day annoyed me.

Emergencies are emergencies and office hours are office hours. That I make myself available on nights and weekends does not mean that I want to be a 24/7 convenience store. But I did call the prescription in, and then I complained to my wife, who replied that I should have ignored the call. If over the years I had not been so compliant, she continued, I wouldn't be getting such calls now. "You brought it on," she said. "You taught her to do this." And I confessed, "I couldn't help it. It's in my bones."

I was paged a second time. A different patient had seen a dentist that morning; the dentist had drained a gum abscess and had prescribed an antibiotic. None of this was a surprise. I had known about the abscess and had talked to the patient about it the night before and to the dentist earlier this day, when she was at his office, giving him relevant particulars about her illness (some drug allergies, but no important issues that altered her dental care). We had agreed on the right drug. She left the dentist's office then paged me because she wanted me to explain the dentist's instructions about the antibiotic. "Take three times daily," he had told her; that's what the label on the bottle said. Why did she page me? To ask me to explain to her why it should be three times daily and not once a day or four times.

I regarded the question as idiotic but kept my cool, "That is the way the medication is normally given," but she wasn't satisfied, and revved herself up to an extended riff about the dentist not being her regular dentist but one covering on the weekend, she didn't like him, didn't like his manner, didn't like the office, and on and on, until, annoyance now evident in my voice, I cut her off, saying that I didn't need to know the details of the dentist's practice today, that three times daily was an appropriate use of the antibiotic, that there was nothing further I needed to do for her today, and that we could follow up next week if need be. Her instant time clashed with my calendar time: I wanted the weekend free. It's in my bones, I guess, always to respond, but not to be cheerful and welcoming every time.

The fact is there are patients I like and patients I do not. I would like to think that I treat them the same, but I am conscious that some annoy me and some do not. Regardless of what I feel, the rules of how we communicate—or, rather, how I respond—are these: How critical is my medical decision, what choices does the patient have, and will she listen to what I have to say. Of course some people are more pleasant than others. Some have unpleasant odors and some do not. Some are coherent and some are not. Some are always pleased while others live in a state of perpetual discontent. But these facts have less to do with how we interact than does my perception of the patient's choice and personal control. The two women described above had the means and mentality to control their "take care of me right now—I don't care what you are doing" impulses; they were not psychiatrically disabled, there was no desperate medical problem involved, but they did not control the impulse. They had fairly trivial needs (as I saw it, but, obviously, not as they did), needs that had to be gratified that instant, and so I was annoyed.

Another patient of mine is a thoroughly unpleasant man, an immigrant with only modest English skills, always complaining bitterly about whomever he has just seen. He never says a pleasant word, and his wife and translator is equally dour. He was seriously disabled, but repeatedly rejected my counsel to help. For two years I had tried to convince him to consider a knee replacement. In the end I succeeded, he had it done, and I went to his bedside after the surgery. His first words of greeting were, "Why did you make me suffer so long?" I wanted to turn on my heel and walk out the door.

I didn't walk out. This man has a crippling arthritis that followed a successful bone marrow transplant for leukemia. He is severely disabled and on Medicaid. There are very few places that can offer him the care that we can, and almost no specialist doctors who will accept him as a patient because of Medicaid. If I don't accept him in my specialist clinic his only other option is to go to a non-specialist clinic in a city hospital with likely less highly tuned skills to care for his very complicated problems. Both his oncologist, at one of the top cancer centers in the world, and I regard him as sufficiently unstable and sufficiently dependent on our care that we keep our personal distaste for this man to ourselves and carry on.

Another patient, recovering from near lethal complications of her illness, called me on a good day twice, on a bad day every hour, often late at night and every weekend, crying hysterically and asking over and over again, compulsively, enervatingly, whether she will ever be well. Even if I were more discrete than I am, this sort of thing one cannot keep secret at home. The phone would ring or the beeper would sound, and my wife would look up and say, "If it's the minister's wife, please take it in the other room." Both the illness and her medication contributed to this patient's very unstable and, I then prayed, transient, psychiatric state. Unpleasant as it was, I answered her questions over and over again, reassured her, many, many times in the months before she at last did improve.

I saw her, again well, the day before I wrote this sentence. She has a very broad smile that dominates her face and a cheery manner that makes everyone like her.

"I'll bet," she said to me yesterday, cheeks and eyes disappearing in that voluminous smile, "that your secretary is glad that I'm well." I bit my lip, restraining myself from saying: "Yep. My wife, too."

Even in complicated circumstances it is a different matter when a patient can exercise free choice. A pleasant, older woman transferred her care to me when her other rheumatologist, a colleague, assumed chairmanship of a department and cut back his practice and asked me to take on her care. Over five years, I gradually weaned her from a dangerous medicine that she had been taking (initially appropriate for her illness, which was now quiescent). Then she developed symptoms that suggested to her that she had a recurrence of her original illness. Without telling me, she went back to her original physician, who saw her but also did not tell me. No big deal. Patients sometimes tire of a doctor and choose another. He re-initiated treatment with the toxic medication.

Some weeks later she came back to me and asked me to take care of the side effects of the medication—the first I learned of the change in plans. She proposed that the other doctor would continue to prescribe the medication and adjust its dose.

I reviewed what had happened and came to a different conclusion. As I listened to her describe her symptoms and interpreted the laboratory tests I thought that she had *not* had recurrence, that my colleague had misdiagnosed her, that the reason for restarting the medication had been wrong, and that other, safer options had been available. I told her I could not take care of her on this medication and that I would discontinue it rather than treat its side effects.

That was not what she wanted. What she wanted, she explained to me, was to continue to see the other physician and receive the medication. My role would be to handle the complications that ensued. He would prescribe, and I would repair.

I couldn't do this, I said, and I refused. Two doctors giving contradictory orders cannot work together. She was operating in clock time: I feel great. I was in calendar time: You are heading for an abyss. Period. End of story.

This is your choice, I said. You can continue to see him (if he prescribes this medication, he can handle the side effects). Or you can see me and not take the medication. In fact, I thought—and said—the other physician had made a terrible mistake.

That I refused to accept her plan appalled her. She was so angry she filed a complaint against me with the administration of our hospital. I in turn was appalled that she felt this way. Nonetheless, I felt then and feel now that my decision was correct. I didn't convince her. She chose to stay with the other physician. He continued the medication and enlisted another doctor, more pliable than I, to manage the side effects.

I have thought about this a lot. I don't think that it was my ego that made me react this way. I do believe that had I agreed with the treatment I would have participated in her care—although I would have insisted on negotiating the dose with the other doctor.

I don't know how it all turned out. I do know that this patient was someone whom I, in effect, fired, because I refused to be party to a course of treatment that I felt to be wrong. She saw my response differently, as callous, irresponsible maybe, and I am sorry for that. But, she had a choice, she knew what she was doing, and she had easy access to other doctors and to other opinions that differed from mine.

A partnership between physician and patient is just that; a request is not a command, and a duty has a context and is not absolute. That I call in a non-emergency prescription on a weekend reflects my personality, as does my feeding Annie at the table. I offer a set of skills but not a convenience store. The other half of the partnership must understand: I do what I can, but I am not at your command. I cannot accede to a course of treatment that I believe will cause harm.

MDL

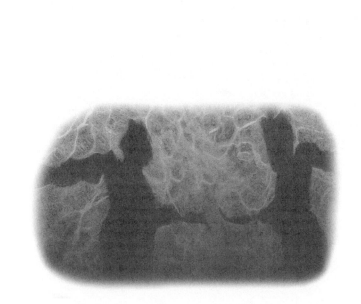

4

Facing the Abyss

Written, Sealed

My doctor and I live in simultaneously overlapping, yet paradoxically, parallel worlds. There are things I will never understand about the scientific underpinnings of the collection of diseases he treats. He can never know the feeling, from inside the body and soul, of one of us who suffers from a disease he understands clinically as both physician and researcher, but has never experienced firsthand. He sees bodies in revolt, systems that respond to drugs and those that do not. Each patient is an individual to him, to be sure, but each also serves as a source of data for current studies that will help those who are now living with illness to overcome it in the future. The information gathered becomes part of a large databank about the complexities of these diseases, which will subsequently become available to generations of physicians and researchers, long after we have left this earth.

In the social sciences as well as in medical research, the populations under study are counted. In social science survey research, findings are stated as accurate generalizations when they can be supported by a properly selected sample of an appropriate size. For example, in the civil liberties survey work I did in the past, we could make a judgment about the incidence of expressed racial intolerance in a particular region of America within an acceptable margin of sampling error. With the letter "N" representing the number of people in a sample, the larger our "N," the more confident we were when stating our conclusions.

I was involved with a team conducting national surveys of American attitudes and opinions, and when the available statistical magic of that time (now quite primitive) was performed on our sample, we felt we could make some definitive and explanatory remarks about what Americans believed about freedom and control, tolerance and intolerance.

The late Professor Herbert McClosky and I co-authored a book, entitled *Dimensions of Tolerance: What Americans Believe About Civil Liberties.* In it we discussed an array of issues about freedom and control in a democracy. However, our overarching question, the fundamental query that drove the entire research design, was quite simple: at what cost freedom, at what loss control?

The question today seems pathetically naïve, in our post-9/11 world, yet I still cling to the notion that more, rather than less, liberty will make us a stronger, and even, perhaps a safer country. What Michael sees when he looks at us as a group is something quite different. He too is looking for random occurrences, but of diseases, in a sample already pre-selected due to the fact that we are all sick. Treatment decisions, not research conclusions, often revolve around the questions of freedom and control as well, but of one's own body, one's ability to maintain dignity, mobility, independence.

In my own lifetime, our conversations have been about the price of controlling the disease through certain drug treatments, which we already know could alter to some extent the nature of who I am. In exchange, I have sometimes, if not frequently, opted for the full freedom of my life, control of my responses, my emotional well being and my intellectual capacity. In social science terms, I have decided from time to time, that the cost of freedom is worth the risk of losing control of the disease.

When I insist I am unable to go forward with my doctor's desired plan, I do so with the knowledge that there have been instances when I have pushed the extreme edge of his tolerance level. Why does my behavior jam up too closely at times to his acceptable comfort level as my physician? Because even in our overlapping worlds, where we come together as doctor and patient, he knows things in a parallel universe that I do not know. He knows the price of freedom in ways that I don't because he lives his life inside an "N"—a population of other chronically sick people. He also knows all the recent research being conducted elsewhere. His life is my illness. My illness is not his life, or is it? Is it not the case that all of us under his care are part of his life, on some level? He knows what happens when a patient insists on total freedom, refuses treatment options, and then finds there is no possibility of stemming the spread of the devastation.

At times, I have made Michael work too hard against my independence and the ferocity of my refusal to take certain drugs, when I am in danger of reaching an abyss that he knows, or at least senses, I am not ready to face. I know what I am doing to him. It greatly saddens me; at times, home alone, I have cried, knowing the stress and tension I have brought into his day and his thoughts when he has returned home. I also know he understands why I can't "give in" immediately, even to his opinion and his direction. I know why we have danced around the issue of clinical trials so many times, then danced away, only to come back. We both know too well my puzzling reactions, even to standard drugs. The risk-benefit is not clear to either one of us; we acknowledge it without needing extended narration. The trust and the intimacy of our relationship render much of that prologue unnecessary, but it hasn't helped us find the answer.

We often negotiate, but even after all these years we can still resort to euphemisms. Sometimes, for instance, we talk about "losing ground." We know what "losing ground" implies; we just don't choose to spell it out. Once or twice, I have pushed him too far, and then he has had no choice but to remind me what it means, in stark and not medically obscure terms. I have surrendered on these occasions. I have given in, not to the disease, but to his wisdom, and to his respect for just how much more I can tolerate on a road to survival.

I have done so because I know that he knows exactly how much I insist, and always will, that I maintain a quality of life that makes it worth the effort to try another treatment strategy. This is the world we jointly inhabit. We are not on the road to recovery or wellness. Together, we are on the road to management and control.

My cousin's beloved husband, a distinguished surgeon, was dying of cancer, when at one point there was a moment of hope. An oncologist told him about experimental treatments that might give him some more time. They said it was a way of managing his particular form of cancer as if it were a chronic disease. There was a passing feeling of euphoria that it was a chronic disease, masquerading as a form of cancer. It wasn't, but he was more than ready to go through the fires of experimental treatment.

However, it was a deadly cancer and he died, after suffering and great anguish. I think about him often; he was that kind of person. He was the kind of man who, once he came into your life, you couldn't imagine him not being there. I particularly think of him as I write this book. I think how bravely he fought to stay alive for my cousin, his great love. I think he must have known that he was really betting against all odds of probability. They were odds that, as a physician himself, he would have understood.

When I feel disgusted with the whole process of my health and the medical roller coaster I am compelled to ride, it is the memory of his determination that makes me fight to continue living, even with disease. However, at other times, even his inspiration isn't enough. The problem with chronic disease is that after a lifetime of it, you reach a point where you really aren't sure what or why you are fighting. The fatigue factor is so enormous; all you want is to be free, even if it means you will live a shorter time. It is as though you want to hear the doctors tell you, "We are going to treat your chronic disease as if it were cancer," which of course, we do, when we go into a variety of forms of chemotherapy protocols.

When I went on an extended round, I felt more like my cousin's husband than I did like myself. I said to myself, if this does not work, I am done. That's it. Over and out.

But, here is the problem. It's a creeping sort of malaise. I think of it as like the kudzu vine. It gums up the workings of your system, but it doesn't take you out at all efficiently. That is when I begin to think about other kinds of endings, ones you take into your own hands. I think about suicide.

After a long period of relentless illness and treatments, with no true remission, I thought about it a good bit. At least, it was something I could choose. I could control my own death, even if I couldn't control the disease, the way I responded to the medications, or the way that others responded to me.

The times I have thought seriously about suicide have always been in the aftershocks of what I call the collateral damage that accompanies chronic illness. As a young girl, when I couldn't sleep due to vastly over-prescribed steroids, I would feel manic, and experience anxiety and panic attacks. Weeks went by when I couldn't sleep at all. I had to stop dance classes. I couldn't run like the wind any longer. I was both filled with hyper-energy and completely exhausted within the same hours.

I hated myself; I wanted to die. I didn't think I was a pretty girl any longer. I felt like a slug. It was the drugs, not even my acknowledgement of the disease, which made me want to die. I remember at about the age of fourteen or fifteen going into the bathroom and looking in the family medicine chest. I read the labels on all the pill bottles prescribed for my mother or father. I recall wondering if I could possibly kill myself if I just took everything in every bottle, in one big gulp. Something stopped me. Even then, there must have been something of the pragmatic researcher in me. I didn't have the facts about the prescriptions. They might not kill me, I reasoned; they might just make me sicker.

Many years later, my mother mysteriously appeared beside my bed during a hospitalization, accompanied by my best friend. I suspected something ominous had happened. My mother has assiduously and meticulously avoided virtually all of my hospitalizations. If she had been summoned, and had agreed to come, it could only mean one thing. When I was discharged, I knew that I would be walking into a house no longer inhabited by a couple, but by a single woman, alone in illness and in heartgrief.

Although the reason for my husband's absence was presumed to be a temporary one, I knew better. The real end of the relationship was ahead of me, just down the road, and I knew it. After I had stabilized, I returned to my job at the university's research center. My colleagues, including very senior professors, threw a party to welcome me back. Everyone was in a festive mood, the dogs of colleagues and students, ever present in those days on campus, were wearing bows and other collar decorations. The word had gotten out that my husband was MIA—or was he AWOL?—Nobody was sure, but they felt that I needed a party. I did not need a party. I needed to wake up into a world where he had stayed by my side, or at least had waited at home for me to return from the hospital. I drove home from the university after the party, with a senior colleague tailing me until I turned off on my street. I pretended I didn't notice him following me home.

What he would never know is that I sat in the driveway of my lovely home, and asked myself if I knew how to gas myself to death in a garage with the car running. I did not. My main dilemma was how to do that and get the garage door closed from the inside. Obviously, I could have figured it out. I thought I was ready to exit, but I wasn't. What had driven me to the brink of serious consideration of suicide was not only the illness, it was the abandonment combined with the disease.

Collateral damage.

As I was turning thirty, I had a particularly dark winter. I was also holding an important job. During the illness and its dramatic developments, at first, I was supported tremendously by my colleagues, especially by my boss and his wife. Then, I had another relapse, a few years later, after they thought they could go off-duty. Not long after that, I was invited to leave. I wasn't exactly fired. It was far too elegant a place to actually fire someone who had written a prize-winning book, and survived a dreadful can-opener lung surgery, and a severe recurrence of illness. I was invited to go elsewhere; but I had no place else to go. They insisted my illness didn't have anything to do with their decision to remove my salary line from the budget. It was an academically-driven place, and I knew well the jealousies and internal fighting for position and status were just as present there, as they were in traditional sholarly settings.

I blamed my illness, which means I blamed myself. What

else could it be? There had not been a bad performance evaluation saying I didn't measure up to the standards required. I thought if I couldn't hold the job that defined my credibility in New York, and that identified me to others and myself as something other than a disease in search of a free person, it was time. Once again, it felt to me like collateral damage. Once again, the concept of "why bother" emerged. I was tired, I was sick again, and I was about to be without a job, and without any medical insurance.

However, the Manhattan of that moment was a place where professional women really looked out for one another. One of my dearest friends, a foundation president herself, whose own mother had committed suicide, clearly had seen the danger signals. Before I knew what was happening, she phoned another woman colleague and I had a lawyer and a fair settlement. Much later I learned it wasn't about me; it was about something else. The president of the institution was having what would eventually become a fairly public affair with a woman whom he wanted to have stay on premises, past her contract. He needed my salary allocation. He had been cheating on his wife who had been by my bedside for months when I was ill. It felt like an act of double-betrayal in my mind, once I found out the truth.

I was not hoping for his death. I was just determined to wait him out. It was not that I hated him for his affair, or for deciding he didn't want me to retain my position. Those were his own choices to make. It was that he had made me believe that I had been unacceptable professionally because I could not be well all the time, even though I tried so hard not to be sick and to work at home when I was.

I do not think of myself as a vindictive person. Close friends have criticized me for being too forgiving and overly generous of spirit, particularly at times when I should be taking care of myself. When he finally died, I carefully clipped the obituary from the paper and, I confess, it was with some relief that I put it in a file drawer. Then, I decided to actually read it and saw that the main achievement listed during his tenure was the program that I had created and directed when I was there.

Many friends across the country, and even in the U.K., called and asked me if I was outraged that the program I had developed and nurtured and administrated had been credited only to him. I said, no, not at all. He was the president of the organization; it was appropriate the research program be remembered as having been created under his leadership. In my heart, I felt that I had won. What it said in his obituary didn't matter to me. I had triumphed over his decision to get rid of me, simply because I had outlived him.

Now, later in life, approaching an age I did not believe I would get within spitting distance of, I think about suicide again. However, now I think of it in far more abstract and intellectual terms. I know that there are things I will not tolerate. There are endings I will not choose. There are drug treatments to which I will no longer subject myself, and new ones I will not experiment with and end up feeling more like a guinea pig than a human being.

I think of what could have happened in a relationship that might have turned out to be life affirming, an intimacy that had the possibility of developing into something I could count on as unique. I become physically numb when I force myself to walk through the steps of how quickly it all came apart—irreparably destroyed—when I could not exhibit enough courage. Drugs and fever made me someone I would not wish to be, and am not. Even though it was carefully explained and he said he accepted what had taken me over, he could never forgive, or forget. Inside a person he had trusted had emerged instead someone he did not know and would not choose to know. Perhaps, he believed that the woman he thought he knew had vanished forever. In other words, the disease had become the woman.

So, I often think, is it better to stop now? These are mental gymnastics—exercises around the universe of theoretical thoughts about life and death. They are different from the thoughts of the young researcher parked in her driveway contemplating the end. Or are they? Again, I have decided, no. Or at least, I have decided, not quite yet. There might come the moment when I do decide to face my life exactly as it stands, and that the "not yet" will become the "yes, now's the time."

I do not know if my doctor knows this about me. We have never talked directly about suicide, not in personal terms. I do not know how many of the rest of us in his circle of patients think these things or might be thinking about them in the real time it takes me to write this paragraph. My guess is that there are more than a few of us engaged in this struggle. I know from talking to other women with chronic illness, who are as attuned to their bodies as I am, that there is a quiet suicide conversation tape, ready to be played in the back of our heads, anytime we choose or feel we need to hear it. We know where the button is and we decide if we are going put it on "play," and listen to it, or not, choosing instead to move to another part of our brain. The part that tells us to read a book, listen to music, go to a museum, see a play, go to a concert, take a walk, call a friend, have a really good dinner, see a film.

We alone can decide this one thing—if we are going to push the button and listen to that end-tape or not. We also decide if we are going to reveal that there is this tape inside our heads. In my case, it is one pre-recorded since my teenage years. We can't decide many things about what will happen in the course of our lives, or what we will be able to do, but if we have that tape in our heads, we decide when, and if, we are going to listen to it. Mine is worn out, filled with rational and irrational hypotheses and strategies about when, and if, and how, and if only. It rewinds, and plays back, as many times as I choose, and then, it is silent.

For now, it remains in the "off" position—until I can't bear the recurrence of disease and the ensuing collateral damage another minute. Then, I push it on again. Until the next time, when I can't stand the notion of thinking in this defeatist way, and promise I will never turn it on again. I promise myself never to think that way again, and I pledge to myself I will not listen to that mental exit tape any longer. I do so knowing what a liar I am.

My doctor knows a series of dark facts we never discuss openly with each other. He knows things I can't know, and don't want to know, because he has been at the ringside seat too many times. He is likely to know what it will look like, or is likely to look like for me, at the end, if I should choose to go forward and let my *katun* "run its course." He has a good idea of how I might die and what amount of suffering I will have to endure. He is also aware that there is a chance that it will somehow really hit my brain in an episode or flare and change my ability to think clearly enough to be able to get out on my own terms. He knows my particular form of disease can take away my eyesight, or a goodly amount of it. I have had that scare, but we talk rarely of that crisis. He has seen us die. He has seen us become completely debilitated. He has seen some of us with other forms of disease become permanent raving lunatics, not just momentary ones, as I had been with fever and drugs.

I assume he has gotten phone calls, from time to time, informing him that one of us has given up, and taken our own exit, in our way, in our own time. These are things we don't talk about. Instead, we talk about just how much longer I will have the freedom to resist, indeed, to refuse, his advice or his next suggested treatment strategy, perhaps even experimental ones. We speak in metaphors and euphemisms. We speak in literary terms, and we speak in references to poetry as well as in medical terminology. Fleetingly, sometimes, we speak as strangers, because I know he knows things I do not want him to tell me. I suspect he knows I think things he would rather not know I think about. At least, not yet.

For Jews, the days of the New Year and the Day of Atonement are the most sacred and the most holy of the entire year. They are called the Days of Awe. I believe for Christians their spiritual importance is similar to the solemnity and sacredness of Holy Week, which includes the Last Supper, the betrayal of Jesus, the Crucifixion and then the Resurrection. For Jews, the Days of Awe are both private days and public days. We must ask those we have harmed for their forgiveness, and then we must ask God (Adonai) to forgive us for what we have done and what we will do. We fast, we pray, we consider the human condition and its fragilities in our public prayers and in our private meditations. We break the fast together and we celebrate and ask for a sweet and good year ahead.

At Rosh Hashanah, as the Days of Awe are just beginning, we pass apples and honey and especially ask that we be blessed with a sweet new year, and that we be inscribed in the Book of Life. In the synagogue, we hear rabbis chant, in Hebrew and in English, "On Rosh Hashanah, it is written, on Yom Kippur, it is sealed, who will live and who will die" [b'rosh hashanah yiketevun, uveyom tzom kipur yehatenmun]. In congregations all over the world we listen or chant along with these ancient and holy words of faith, of heritage.

I think the words mean something very different for me than they might for some of my friends or to the families who surround me at High Holiday services. Even before I knew those words, I was keenly aware of the concept of this ethereal book and the metaphor of the inscription for those who will live and those who will die. It reminds me we are all at risk. Life and death are random for each of us. I feel less control only because I know more about what is going on inside me than the person in the pew in front of me probably knows. The words terrify me but they also provide comfort. They comfort me because they make me feel that I am a part of the larger human condition and not, due to my illness, apart from others.

I have been depressed. I have been close to the edge of the abyss. Perhaps I have danced on the ridge just above its depths. I have thought it not worth holding down the fort any longer for "the battle at the isle of self" but every year when I hear those words—I return to a childhood dream of wellness, of living a regular and a normal life. I say to myself, quietly, in the place in my brain that is far from the suicide tape section, "me too, please, I want to be inscribed in the book of life for a healthy New Year."

Perhaps it is the case, that although we have never said it to each other, Michael, my doctor, lets me dance my dance of defiance and denial because he knows that I continue to want to be included in that inscription each autumn. He understands I still have the dreams of a healthy woman. I also think he knows, that despite a lifetime of being ill, I always choose life, at least for now.—And when the time comes that I don't, or I can't, we will even talk about this eventuality. When it is time, if that time comes.

AB

The Games Are Over

I know that Alida thinks about suicide. I know that other patients do as well. Do they tell me? Or, can I tell if suicide is on someone's mind?

Yes, I probably can. What is less clear to me is whether I tell myself what I see. Patients give me clues. Sometimes, and sometimes not, I read these clues. I may or may not choose to act. My choice may or may not be voluntary. Instinct and practicality tend to rule—will my acting make a difference at all? Or it may be that hindsight gives clarity, and I discover that, being in the moment, I was blind to the warning signs.

Every hospital has its rainmaker, a doctor whose practice caters to famous and very rich patients, people who give very large donations and whose names are carved in marble on its walls. A rainmaker's secret is that his office is run with the courtesy of a royal palace and the security of the Pentagon. In such offices people with large demands find satisfactory accommodation of their needs. A less visible secret of the rainmaker's office is she who guards the door.

I first encountered this world as a young physician when I was summoned by such a guard—not asked, not begged, but summoned—to come personally to the rainmaker's office, a house call, as it were, to consult on a client who did not wish to appear in public with his current complaint. (It didn't work: I hospitalized the patient that day, albeit in a very private suite.) The lady in command of the office was tall and imperious. Her name and accent implied German birth. She had a rigid, severe manner and she was in total control.

I went to the office, was formally identified (I was asked to show my identification badge!), ushered in, directed to the proper place, and, concluding my business, escorted out, all paper work done, efficiently, respectfully, and with dispatch. Also, without humor. That was a bit of a surprise—this particular rainmaker has a sense of humor that is well known. The jokes apparently did not apply to his office when sensitive issues were in play. I was a bit intimidated by the experience, especially by the guard, who towered over me.

Over the years I had other dealings with that office. I would receive such a summons about once a year. With more experience and a few added years I gained confidence to hold my aplomb more easily, even though the imperatrix at the door remained the same. At least she recognized me now. Still, she would initiate the call to my office, my secretary would tell me that Dr. X wanted to speak to me, I would pick up the telephone, and I would hear her command, forceful, non-negotiable, accent and tone reminiscent of the actor portraying someone on the wrong side in a grade B World War II movie: "Yust a moment, I vill get Dr. X for you now," this at a time of my life when I expected people to wait for me; but I knew the game and I would wait until he spoke. No matter the urgency, he always began a conversation with one or two jokes. Quite a contrast between the rainmaker and his gatekeeper. I could stand back from the moment. I was used to the style. We all got along.

Years later I got to know the guard from a different side. She was elderly and semi-retired; when she developed severe rheumatoid arthritis, the rainmaker asked me to oversee her care. I then learned that she was Swiss and not German, and that her first language was French (her accent still sounded German to me). I also found out that she was widowed for just a few years and that her only child, a girl, a doctor, had killed herself shortly before. I learned that she read French classics and delighted in contemporary art. She often visited

Switzerland where her two brothers, one a twin, still lived. I didn't really know the rest. My impression is that no one dear was near, or among the living.

Outside her command post she was not imperious at all. Rather, she was gentle and self-effacing, apologetic when she thought a request of hers might be difficult to fill. I enjoyed my conversations with her. She wanted to banter in French, often did, but my knowledge of that language is very formal. She had a sense of humor and often made jokes in her more colloquial style; I tended to miss the point.

I was not able to help her. Her diagnosis and treatment plan were straightforward, but there are patients who simply do not respond to the medications we use. I prescribed first the gentle medicines, then the more powerful, then the even more powerful, then even the new miracle drugs, but the arthritis kept marching on, destroying joint after joint, making her progressively disabled. Hands and wrists, shoulders and knees, swollen and damaged, turned her life into one of unremitting pain. Friends, she said, helped her cope at home.

Then a spinal disk pinched a nerve, adding a new, constant burning pain down her leg and preventing her from walking more than a few steps at a time. The usual palliatives did not work so we opted for surgery to remove the disk. That gave her relief for a while, but the pain came back. A repeat MRI scan showed a little bone fragment that had been missed with the first surgery. It now pressed on the nerve again. She scheduled a second surgery to remove the fragment.

On the day the second surgery was scheduled she developed fever and abdominal pain. I was urgently paged to see her in the pre-operative holding area. I suspected, then confirmed, inflammation of a little weak spot on her bowel. I cancelled the back surgery and transferred her to a medical floor. We administered antibiotics but her pain and fever worsened. I called in an abdominal surgeon who operated and repaired the problem. Her post-operative course was somewhat stormy. Hands disabled, sciatica unimproved, she now had a colostomy as well. She was unable to care for herself, so we sent her to a nursing facility to heal—this was the first time in her life, I believe, that she did not control the rules. She stayed at the nursing home for several months then came back to have the colostomy closed. The arthritis and the sciatica remained unchanged. After the procedure she returned to her apartment, a visiting nurse checking in from time to time, and, with an assistant, she was able to come to my office for follow-up care.

She asked if I thought she would ever be independent again. I said no, I doubted that she could be independent again. She asked if I foresaw a cure, would the inflammation subside, would the pain go away. I did not foresee a cure. I gave her medication for pain. I could do that, I could do it generously, but I could do little more.

On one visit at about this time she brought a gift for me: a four-volume *Club de Librairie de France* special edition of E.T.A. Hoffmann's *Contes et Dessins* (Tales and Sketches), in French, printed in 1956, an edition of 7,500, of which this set was number 2,699. It was a thoughtful gift. We had discussed these tales and the Offenbach opera *Tales of Hoffman* as well, though how and when the conversation took place I do not recall. "I always loved these stories," she said, "but I cannot read them anymore. I know that you will enjoy them as much as I did." The past tense verb meant nothing to me at the time.

Doctors use the term "train wreck" to describe an unstoppable catastrophe, and "impending train wreck" to describe a foreseeable one they likely cannot prevent. Something about this gift might have suggested an impending train wreck but

I did not tumble to the clue. I took the gesture at face value, a kind act and a pleasure of sharing an intellectual adventure that one had enjoyed. I suppose I had an inchoate sense of unease. After all, I knew her fairly well. I also know what acts of closure mean. But I felt myself paralyzed and unable to see beyond the surface of the act. Very likely I did not want to consider where a more thoughtful look might lead. She was seventy-eight, dependent on others, severely disabled, in pain and living alone. Or maybe I did understand and was resigned and fatalistic: I did not know of anything else that I could do except continue the medication for pain.

Several weeks later the rainmaker's partner called. An ambulance had brought her to our emergency room, he said. She was dead when the ambulance arrived. A visiting nurse or a neighbor had found her unconscious at home and had called 911.

There was no autopsy. No blood tests for toxic substances were done. The death certificate, signed by the doctor in the ER, said pneumonia was the cause.

I did not ask how many pain pills from her recently renewed prescription remained in her apartment. I had no need to know. I did not want to know. Actually, I'm pretty sure that I do know, but there is no point in telling anyone now.

In the Offenbach opera, *Tales of Hoffman,* toward the end of her act, Giulietta sings:

> …without pause the fatal wheel
> does its turns,
> faces are somber
> the whole world sad,
> the games are over…

MDL

Death

Death begins with a telephone call. This is a marked point in time. From that moment on, events move backwards and forwards simultaneously. From this single moment events, rather than judgments, assume control. A moment ago I was a doctor in charge. Now I am a bystander, a commentator, a narrator on a stage, a translator for those whose eyes have less experience to see. Nonetheless I am a participant, thought by the other participants to have magical powers, but lacking them utterly, and rarely able to confess how little I can do.

Late on a cold December afternoon, a friend and patient, age fifty-three, nurse and professor, walking down the street with her husband, collapsed a few hundred feet from the emergency room of a small neighborhood hospital that she knew. Immediately diagnosed by the emergency room physicians to be in cardiac arrest, she was resuscitated and transferred to a larger hospital uptown. Her husband had been at her side, and had been able to engineer immediate care. "Call them," he pleaded with me on the telephone, "Tell them about her. Come."

What to tell? The images in my mind flashed backward from this moment. I had known her longer than he had. I met her more than a quarter-century ago, during her student days, when she was no more than twenty-five. I first saw—and hospitalized—her as a young woman with a high fever, watched her recover, return to her job, meet other men, then meet and wed the man now hysterically calling me on the telephone. I had seen her through a few bad times and many good times as well, managed her illness through her only (and troubled) pregnancy, shared with her the joys of her son's growth, his schooling, his bar mitzvah, his success in his first year in college.

Over this long period she and I spoke of private things, as patients and doctors do: problems with parents, frustrations at home, during which she started and stopped smoking, then started and stopped again. It worried me that she smoked. She had had a heart problem before, and her cardiologist was concerned as well.

These were the images in my mind, but surely that is not what her husband was asking me to say. He wanted me to explain to the intensive care unit doctors all about the prosaic, mechanical things: the nature of her illness, the medication she was on, the allergies about which I knew. He did not expect me to, nor would I tell them the intimate details of the person I knew her to be.

Had we—she and I—known that this moment would come? Of course, we had. In her profession, an intensive care unit nurse herself, she knew the sickest patients, and was quite familiar with the processes of death. She had had reflective moments; she had told me how she expected to die. The scenario she envisioned was not unlike the events of this day. We could not have predicted the time or the place.

She knew and had outlined those procedures that she would not permit if she were able to exert control. There was no formal living will, but rather a pact between her and me (and, I assume, her husband as well). She had always been certain of this. Nineteen years before, when her newborn son was sent against her request to the neonatal intensive care unit, she had set the rules, had even gone directly to the Chief of Staff, to get her wishes obeyed.

Although she was a good deal younger than I, she had assumed that she would die while still under my care. She had told me several times that, at the end, I would have no miracles to give. She knew very well the limits of medical power. She asked only that I protect her from the end-of-life indignities that she so despised.

I went to her hospital as soon as I could. I was expected, her husband had made the contacts, and formalities were waived. The staff of the floor allowed me access to her records and permitted me to write a note. These were necessary protocols because I was not on staff in that hospital.

The note I wrote was *pro forma*. I had no new insights and had no new suggestions that would change her course. I had instantly seen that she was going to die: short, inadequate breaths; pulse on the monitor much too fast; lips and hands dusky, hands and feet cold as blood vessels went into spasm to handle low blood flow; face lacking color and tone; eyes struggling to focus and make sense of this world. It is a look all doctors have seen before. I don't know whether my face mirrored what I saw—I'm sometimes not as inexpressive as I would like.

But all that is irrelevant. "I'm not going to make it, am I?" she whispered to me. I do not always tell patients the full truth, but I do not lie to a direct question. I could not do so if I tried.

"We need you to try," I answered. "We need *you*," but I did not deny what she had said.

Exhausted, she squeezed my hand for a long while, looked directly at me, smiled a wry smile and shook her head. She was falling asleep. "I'll come back," I said. But she did not waken and I did not return.

Memory fails, but I think it was her husband who called to tell me that she had died. I went to the funeral service and to a memorial service at a later time. I later sat down with her husband

and with her son purportedly to discuss the medical events; but, of course, we discussed her life instead. She had achieved more than others do with double the years, we said, and she had gone in the way that she chose.

Three months later, I was back in the same intensive care unit watching another patient die. This was a youngster, an only child, a miracle child, her parents said, who had appeared after many infertile years. She had been a happy child who had fallen ill while in high school, in California, had recovered, though not fully, and, strong-willed, announced that she would leave California—and, I imagine she thought, illness—behind. (Was this child following Alida's steps, or telling me what I needed to write?) She applied to and was accepted by a college in New York. With her parents' and doctor's permission she headed east, with a note to me from her doctors at home.

I was a bit appalled when I met her. She was much more ill than I had surmised. Very self-possessed as well, "I expect my doctors to wash their hands before they touch me," she said on our first encounter, almost before we said hello, catching me by surprise. I had not thought until then of the sociological value of washing one's hands before rather than after the exam.

The two years that I knew her were touch and go. She was too ill from the first to continue; she took a leave of absence, returned home, part way through her freshman year. The California doctors resumed her care, patched her up to some extent, and sent her back to New York. Returned, she was a fireball, joining organizations, living a freshman's life to the full, traveling to Boston and New Orleans as a school representative, ducking doctor's appointments whenever she could, and stopping medications when they interfered.

When I did see her, things did not look good. Her blood pressure was rising, her blood count falling, her kidneys failing.

I called her back from her dorm, read her a medical riot act, and pulled my trump card. "I don't care what you believe, I don't care what the other doctors said, you're going to be on dialysis very soon unless we act right now." Everything is negotiable until it is not, and I will tell you when that is. We had passed the negotiating point.

My insistence brought tears. There were telephone calls back and forth to California and one horrible moment when she called me, incoherently, in the middle of the night, defenses down, terrified. I had not previously seen her lose control. I was so disturbed I called her parents to ask about her change of mood, but they thought I had just seen a part of her personality that she had kept hidden from me. At first, she resisted the aggressive treatment that I proposed, then after consulting with her parents, she finally acceded, and we went ahead. The treatment, an intravenous infusion of a powerful but toxic medicine, passed without event, and her anxiety eased.

A few weeks later, my beeper went off at a late hour. The beeper screen tells me the number to call, much like cell phones do today, and the answering service always presents a brief message as well, like a text message. The beeper is activated through a telephone line, by dialing a telephone number. Wrong numbers occur fairly often.

This night the screen presented a number that I did not recognize and there was no message, so I did not return the call. Twenty minutes later the beeper chirped again. It was the same number and this time I did call. The number turned out to be the cell phone of my patient's roommate. (How they had my beeper number is not clear to me; I may have given it to her for one time use when I had been expecting to hear from her, while someone else was taking my calls.) My patient had become short of breath very suddenly. Her roommate had taken her directly to the emergency room near to her dorm.

Almost as soon as she had arrived in the emergency room, she stopped breathing. Emergency measures had been applied, but oxygen did not get to her brain for a long time. I learned later that she had spent the evening calling her mother in California, telling her how sick she was, but not calling me. That news was upsetting. Those few hours, maybe even the twenty minutes lost with the beeper, might have made a difference, I think. But, of course I will never know.

And here I was, back in the same intensive care unit of this unfamiliar hospital, staring at this beautiful young girl, not yet nineteen, on life support, likely brain-dead. A small ebony face, usually highly animated but now relaxed and peaceful, shrouded in hospital white sheets, the corrugated pastel blue breathing tube slowly oscillating off to the side, little dark hands emerging from underneath the sheets, providing the only color in the room, clear plastic intravenous lines invading their space, a quiet scene, a painterly scene, were its implications not so hellish.

The anguish in my heart reflected in her parents' eyes. We, her parents, the patient, and I, had talked of illness but not of death. She had fled the land of illness to live a normal life, and we were all unprepared.

Her dream had been an illusion. In our last encounter I had threatened her and had exorcised her dream. I forced on her—not really, she consented, but I know that I coerced—the treatment she dreaded.

Did she now lie here unconscious because she had submitted to my importuning and had not done it her way? Because I had waited too long to intervene? Is it because I had destroyed her dream, or broken her will, that she did not call?

MDL

Out Of Sync

In my early thirties, not long after my diagnosis with Wegener's and still not fully recovered, I received an emergency phone call from my father that a lump had been detected in my mother's routine mammography. My mother was, at that time, in her middle seventies. Though her life had been constantly awash in any number of fears, justified and otherwise, she certainly had reason to be fearful of this: her mother had died in her early sixties of breast cancer.

However, she refused a biopsy, and my father was lost and in a panic about how to persuade her to agree to the procedure. Somehow, I managed to pull myself together and fly to California from New York to assist. Friends of my parents picked me up at the LAX airport. Their faces told me they had a story I wasn't ready to hear.

It was in fact a story I didn't want to hear, but it wasn't about my mother. Between my father's earlier frantic telephone call earlier that day and my arrival, he had been rushed to the hospital with internal bleeding. We went straight to the hospital where I found him somewhat dazed and desperately frightened. A Southern man of a certain generation, he was suspicious of all doctors, but especially hospitals, where, according to his belief system, people only went to die. He had been born at home, and with the exception of dental work, had never been in a hospital or had any surgery. I walked in to see him and found my mother sitting at the bed, her anxiety palpable enough to register on the Richter scale.

The doctor treating my dad had told my mother that he suspected colon cancer, and a series of invasive tests were scheduled for the next morning. I also learned that my mother's friend had scheduled her biopsy for the next morning without telling her, and was prepared to do whatever was needed to get her to the appointment. That left me in charge of my father. When the physician arrived to talk to us about the procedures, my father turned his head to the wall and said that this was his daughter's terrain. I asked him what he meant by that, and he said I knew about doctors and tests and hospitals, and I should arrange everything. He wanted to know nothing about what was going to happen to him. He also insisted that if it were cancer, he would decline all treatment, and just "fold down."

I asked the doctor if I could speak to him privately. Having dealt with my mother all day, this physician had somehow maintained his humanity and his composure. But, as we left my father's room, I threw what must have seemed a hand grenade at him. I did not mince words. I told him I was quite ill myself, and in fact was taking some fairly rough drugs and was worried about cracking up under the possibility of having two parents diagnosed with cancer at the same time. He looked at me in surprise; I must have looked absolutely normal to him.

What could be wrong with me, he asked, after first assuming I was their grandchild. I told him I had *Wegener's Granulomatosis,* and that it was in an active phase. He looked at me in complete disbelief. I had this attention-grabbing disease and there I was, alone, of course, an only child, dealing with two difficult and childish older parents. You need some Valium he said, after he regained his equilibrium. "Can you take it?" I said I would call my doctor, but that I was pretty sure I could take it.

The next days were a kaleidoscope of images from hell. My mother had her biopsy and it was diagnosed as cancer. By the time the oncologist made that call to me, or rather came to find me, I was waiting in the family room to find out just how extensive my father's by-then-diagnosed colon cancer was.

Mother's doctor said he thought it would be a good idea if I had someone with me when I returned to my parents' home to tell her the news. I told him I didn't think I needed anyone with me, and that I would wait until I found out about my father. I asked the oncologist how long it would take to have my mother's surgery. He had already contacted the breast surgeon; her surgery would be the following morning, when presumably my father would either be in intensive care, or on his way up the Celestial Staircase. The physician attending my father had informed the oncologist that I had Wegener's. He said "who is taking care of you through this?" His question was like a smack in the face.

Taking care of me? What a concept I thought. I told him it was no problem: I had been my mother's caretaker, consoler and mother for years, but my father being sick was a pretty big deal. He asked about siblings, about a husband, about family. I gave all those answers that doctors must hate to hear, and then I looked in his eyes and I reverted to type. I started to tell him that he should not be concerned, "I am as tough as dirt," I heard myself saying, "Don't worry about me." In that moment, I realized I was in fact what I had said I was.

The surgeon came in a bit later and told me that my father's cancer was in a very early stage; he was able to resect the colon. The cancer had been encapsulated, but he would have to be very careful about his diet, and he would be having follow-up appointments. He said I should hire a private nurse for my father. I told him there was not money for anything like that. He arranged for a visiting nurse to come by once a day under the hospital's plan that did not require extra funds, and was in fact covered by a far more generous Medicare plan than we have now.

When I got back to the house, my mother was asleep in

their bedroom, surrounded by her totems: prayer books and devotional materials from a variety of faiths; a statue of the Virgin Mary that her friend, a Roman Catholic, had placed next to her bed; and countless volumes of poetry—her true prayer books. I woke her gently and told her the good news about my father, which she took as his death sentence nonetheless. She was of the generation that still called cancer "C-A."

Then, I braced myself for the task ahead, and told her that her biopsy had not shown what we had hoped, that the lump did contain cancer cells and that we needed to pack her up and get her to the hospital. She looked at me for a time and then, without warning, her hand flew out and she slapped me across the face as hard as she could, "You are a liar." And she began to sob and wail, not to any God, but to her mother, who had been dead for at least forty years. I noticed that she had a candle burning at the portrait-shrine to her mother, which was always on her dresser.

I might have been tough as dirt, but I had hit the bottom of a very deep ditch. I walked out of the bedroom without a word and headed down to her friend's a few houses away. Without drama, I told her the diagnosis and how my mother had behaved. I said I was officially off-duty with my mother and could she help? She then told me that she had been raised in an orphanage, having been given up by her mother, and that my mother was like a real mother to her. They also had both lost a son, and therefore shared a strong bond.

Without family, and as ill as I was, I realized that here was, to my surprise, a woman willing to become the daughter to my mother so that I could be the daughter to my father. Within days, my parents made hospital history, as the administration had moved them into the same room. This was unheard of then, but subsequently during their many illnesses and traumas,

I have always arranged for this immediately, knowing very well the outcome if it were otherwise. My parents work in tandem; when one is sick the other becomes sick or falls down with subsequent injuries requiring hospitalization. As I write these words about caring for others when ill, I marvel that I was that sick child, who so feared that my very older parents would die and leave me all alone.

Tough as dirt? Well, maybe not so tough any longer, but resilient and accepting. This is the way in which my life has played out. When my parents were both in the cancer crisis, I had a moment or more of great wallowing self-pity, because as I was constantly coming back and forth to the hospital, women my very age were coming in with husbands to deliver their babies. Or worse, leaving the hospital, radiant with tiny bundles wrapped in pink or blue in their arms. I remember thinking that I was the one that was totally "out of sync" with my generation. Shouldn't I be coming into a hospital to have a baby, not leaving a hospital in New York, with my chest taped up from lung surgery, then shortly thereafter have to rush off to yet another hospital in California in order to care for both parents afflicted with cancer at the same time. But, such was and is my peculiar world. Here I was, dealing with parents old enough to be my grandparents, while everyone else seemed to me, in that surreal sequence, to be having babies in the normal rhythm of life. I choked back tears for myself and then decided I had better just get on with it. Reality has the transforming ability to trump fantasy visions of the life unlived or unattainable.

Before my parents were released, the lovely physician that had been my father's primary doctor came to say good-bye to me. I told him that my father would never follow any diet whatsoever, and it was probably foolish to try to persuade him. He said he had already figured that out, but gave me the list of all the things he must not eat. I believe my father began to eat most of them within days, his own act of defiance, perhaps? Chocolate headed the list of forbidden foods; his reply was that he would rather die than never eat chocolate again—an assertion that many might agree with, in point of fact. Soon, he would rather die than not eat an almond or a cashew or an olive. The day I was leaving the hospital, helped by the escort service, with both of them in wheelchairs, the doctor caught up with me and gave me a kiss on the cheek, an unusually friendly gesture and one I very much appreciated. He said, "How on earth do you do this, I mean really, how can you do this with these two, when you are sick?"

I smiled and said to him, "What are my options?" He said others might well choose many other options. I said perhaps so, but they were not options I ever thought about.

After I closed down the pity-party for Alida, I realized I was grateful I was not pregnant and did not have small children. I simply would not have had the energy to deal with children and my parents at the same time. But, I know that I would have tried, and that would undoubtedly have proven a spectacular disaster.

In the past few years, I have watched older friends of mine deal with aging parents, difficult or sick adult children, and ill grandchildren. Even well, it is not really the sandwich generation, as the press likes to call it; it is a crowded, hot subway rush hour of life's complexities. Not knowing the experience of motherhood, I nonetheless think about it often. As I mentioned earlier in this book, when I began my career as a patient, all the doctors were men, at a time when virtually all women stayed home and took care of their husbands, their families, and their homes. The doctors treating the chronically ill had support at home as well, actual and emotional.

Now, I see many women doctors, and in rheumatology in particular the gender map has changed. There is a continent full of women rheumatologists, many of them mothers. So they have a different set of things that get thrown into the "vacuum nature abhors." They treat ill people, and come home to children of their own with needs and illnesses, and in some cases, these are female rheumatologists who also have chronic illness, even autoimmune illness. I hope they are as tough as dirt or have lots of totems to guard against their battle fatigue. Mostly, I hope they have a strong net underneath to catch them if they fall.

In our time, with increased longevity, and women working and living as physicians and mothers, nobody is really out of sync any longer. We are all in a place where we must often put our own needs and our own sickness to the side, and get on with the business of being fully engaged, as mothers, wives, doctors, lovers, employees or employers, and yes, as the parents of parents who can't take care of themselves any longer.

My father might well have scorned the forbidden food list and survived, and he has so far. It was, however, a theme that would replay in my life in an odd way. During my earliest days in New York, I found my mother-mother. That mother you dream about; the storybook mother who argues with the night staff at the hospital because you don't have enough blankets. That mother who sits by your bed reading to you and engaging your mind, that mother who brings you treats, and gossip and unconditional love. I found her in the person of the anthropologist Professor Dame Mary Douglas. She and I were at the same research institution in New York. The Sisters of the Sacred Heart had raised her because her mother had died when she was a very young girl, and her father had placed her and her younger sister in a convent school outside of London.

Out of sync no longer, my life had an incredible synchronicity to it. Just as my mother's younger Roman Catholic friend had become her surrogate daughter, an older Roman Catholic woman became my surrogate mother, protector, muse, mentor and intellectual guide. She loved the story of my father refusing to abide by the doctor's list of forbidden foods. Her earliest work had been on forbidden foods of the Lele tribe in the Congo. Mary was always there as my mother in situ until her last days, although by then she had moved back to London; I visited often, and was with her months before her death in the spring of 2007. Knowing her diagnosis was a form of cancer she could not beat, I wanted to do something for her. I wanted to mother her.

She would not have it. We went to the theater, we ate at wonderful restaurants, and we talked about how much time she had and which of the last books she could get done before she died. She straightened me out about where I was heading with my own work, and she had a serious talk with me about the next five years of my life and what I needed to do, personally and professionally. We gossiped. We went to Oxford and she took me around to every important location from her student days where she had also met her lifelong companion and husband, James, who had died a couple of years earlier. We talked about my disease. She taught me about Judaism, as she had become a scholar of Hebraic texts, while remaining a devout Catholic. She was the perfect Jewish non-Jewish Mother. And then, she left me; she left all of us, especially her three beloved real children and adoring grandchildren. Her own grown children, close to my age, were so aware of my connection to her that they included me in her funeral, as a family member.

It turns out that even if it comes very late, being mothered is never too late in the game of life. The maternal balm she had applied for three decades had worked for me. I wondered about how Mary had managed all those years with the mother-loss in her own life, and then I looked at her daughter Janet's eyes during the funeral Mass in London. I did not jump in and try to mother Janet but I tried then, and continue to try to be a good friend, and hopefully, an older sister of choice.

Out of sync and in sync, all at the same time.

Thinking of Mary and of illness and death and family and responsibilities and whether one takes the moral road or the lesser one, I think that it is all about choosing to live. I believe that, while chronically ill, it is about making it come together for yourself and for those who are in your care, whether in the normal range of things or in the more unconventional, as in my case. If my father's doctor were still around and asked me how I did it, now I would have a different answer. I would quote from one of the "chapters" of the Tao of Lao Tzu, the Ursula le Guin version:

> Knowing other people is intelligence,
> Knowing yourself is wisdom
> Overcoming others takes strength
> Overcoming yourself takes greatness.
> Contentment is wealth.
> —To live until you die
> Is to live long enough.

As I read these words, I know finally that in this out-of-sync life of mine, everything has been absolutely in sync.

AB

Nature Abhors a Vacuum

I don't suppose that Aristotle foresaw that his thought, "nature abhors a vacuum," would, after two and a half millennia, become a cliché. I also don't suppose that Aristotle, the Greek, would want to know that I tried to find the correct citation by hunting in Latin (*natura abhorret vacuum*). Greek? Latin? Were they even really Aristotle's words?

I looked up the Latin phrase, *horror vacui.* I found that it is, indeed, attributed to Aristotle, but it mostly refers to a 17th century experiment in the German town of Magdeburg, where Otto von Guericke sealed the edges of two half-spheres of copper with grease, fit the edges together to make a globe, and, using a valve, pumped out the air from inside. The air outside the globe held the halves together so strongly that teams of horses could not separate them—until von Guericke opened the valve and air rushed in. Though the experiment proved that air has weight, we remember the nature/vacuum part. Another part of the story is not mentioned at all. The shells were not crushed. A very strong solid inside the hemispheres could have withstood the force as well.

I told Alida I was drafting a chapter about the "sandwich generation," about those patients who are torn between their children's needs and those of their parents. A metaphor had popped into my head—*horror vacui,* in Latin, to describe this current sociological phenomenon.

"Nature abhors a vacuum" is a platitude, a metaphor about life. We don't live in a vacuum, we say. The outside world will always rush in—for good or ill. If you are in the middle of your own health crisis and need others to help, they may be there for you. But, sometimes you can be in crisis and the outside will continue to assault you with its demands.

As hurricane winds try to gain access to the near vacuum at the center of the storm, so does the outside world try to invade your personal space. No matter how ill you may be, a parent, a child, a sibling, a spouse, can lay a claim on you. You need, you want, you require someone to assist you, yet someone to whom you are tied makes demands. That person's needs—as he perceives them—have priority over yours. You are a care-seeker but you are expected at the same time to be a caregiver.

This push-pull is evident in my office every day. Here is what I can do. I can reason with the family, point out that my patient is not strong enough to take on an additional mental, emotional, physical load. Perhaps I can ask the others to ease off a bit, possibly I can point out that she is exhausted and cannot take on new roles. Usually my patient does not have much control, and chooses, or is forced, or tries to perform the pre-assigned family role. She tries to respond, and feels guilty if she cannot. Caught between her own needs and those of loved ones to whom she is tied, she tries to ignore the pain, to function as if normal again, and ends up exhausting herself in return.

Here are a few stories of people who came to my office just this week:

A twenty-five year-old woman, lying on a stretcher, waiting to be admitted to our hospital, said: "Please don't tell my father. He has enough to worry about." And what does her father worry about? "My patient's sixteen year-old sister has been comatose, on life support, for four months; the doctors are asking to 'pull the plug,' call her brain-dead, and let her die. My patient's parents are divorced." The mother says yes and the father says no. Curled in a fetal position in my examining room, with a temperature of 104°, my patient is the go-between, worried that *she* is adding to *their* stress.

A fifty-seven year-old woman, wheelchair-bound, cannot walk or feed or dress herself because she has had crippling arthritis since her teen years. Her mother is dying of cancer. The patient's sister is estranged, uninvolved, and will not assist. "My mean sister," my patient calls her, "my useless sister." Then, in tears, she asks me for a tranquilizer. "My mother and I are so close. I've got to help her in her last days."

A thirty-two year-old woman has severe, recurring arthritis that incapacitates her about three days out of the week but eases up enough to allow limited function on other days. Her five-year-old only child is autistic. She takes the child to special programs—when she can. Her husband has recently been diagnosed as dysfunctional due to his own attention deficit disorder. Her insurer sent a detective to videotape her wheeling her child to the treatment center to prove that she can walk and therefore does not need disability support. "But," she says, "I have to be there for my son."

I think of these things because Alida is in one of those bad times, in fact is quite ill, but is trying to assist her elderly parents, who have their own needs and cannot respond to hers. The outside pressure rushes in. Yet much resilience remains.

Nature abhors a vacuum? No ill person lives in that vacuum. Responsibilities do not stop. Whether a family is close-knit or dispersed, whether financial or social resources are great or small, the platitude predicts: someone to whom my patient feels responsible will say, "My priorities always trump yours." My patient, no matter how ill, will try to respond. Can her guilt be less? Can her effort be more? It is really hard to tell.

I listen to the part of the tale that she shares with me. I can mobilize some resources. I ask our hospital to provide social service support. I recount anecdotes that I hope will help her organize a self-protective plan. I don't know that my efforts do very much. Nature's laws will be obeyed. Outside forces will try to crush the shell.

So we work to strengthen the shell, to make her personal shield stronger than the copper hemispheres, to keep the outside forces out, to support her to be sure that she remains hard like the diamond in the center that can be compressed no more.

Nature takes advantage of weakness to control what it can reach. If the shell can be kept strong, nature will let the vacuum be. Time will pass, the winds outside the shell will subside, and the pressure difference between the outside and the inside will eventually cease.

MDL

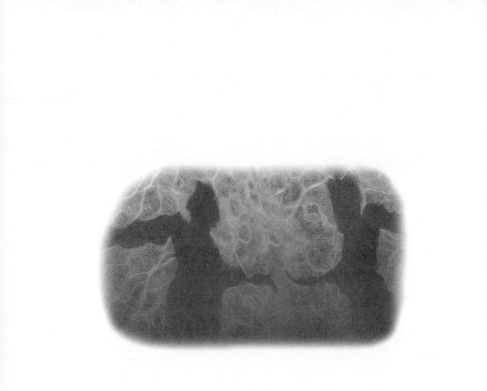

5

Spring Returns

The Puzzle Pieces of Life

Just as the seasons change, the severity and frequency of the episodes of chronic illness within an individual person's life change dramatically. Chronic illness is a lifelong experience of dark storms and then quite unexpected blossoms.

Doctor and patient, each in our own way, strive to understand and attempt to conquer a collection of diseases that at times seem far more intelligent than the most advanced research, and more determined than the most gritty and resolute patient. Some of us will win this war, and experience a lasting period of peace. Many of us will not.

Even for those of us who lose the war against the unwanted and uninvited invaders, we are not defeated. We still have days filled with experiences other than illness. As I have aged along with the condition and status of my illness, I have come to feel that struggle itself is a victory. Because of its unusual nature, there are daily triumphs as we strive to define ourselves apart from disease and its demands. Inevitably, some of us will not see anything at all like a full *katun* play out before leaving. For those who have only just begun to inhabit this other country, parts of this book might be frightening. Hopefully, there is still truth in the adage that in knowledge there is power.

As doctors mature in both their years and professional careers, there will be seasons when they will see more, rather than fewer, of us exit. I think about the younger physicians. I hope they will not become hardened, but know that eventually they must become resigned to the fact not all of us die at "acceptable" ages. As doctors in the field of chronic illness they see their patients more often than doctors in other specialties or in general practice. At the end of their medical careers, by virtue of their choices, they have been part-time residents on this alien planet. I think of their hearts, and of how much they must constrict their feelings in the face of loss in order to continue on helping us, and how they must find a way to absorb what might well be perceived as failures.

Chronically ill people do not just live in a place that is different; our own bodies imprison us because our internal systems so wrongly understand us. For me, the best description of what it means to be chronically ill one's whole life is in Janet L. Hopson's title for her article that appeared in *Science* magazine, *Battle at the Isle of Self*. How better to summarize the ongoing internal warfare? Our bodies are unable to correct the faulty code of enemy and friend in the conversation between cell, tissue and organ. We are threatened by our own interior workings—we are literally caught in the crossfire raging inside of us.

As the Italians say about love, "if there are flowers, they will bloom." We continue on but we are stuck in the same body, hoping for a spring, which might provide us with real blossoms. As patient only, I finally have forgiven my weary body for its personal betrayals and disappointments. I have coped at times quite well, sometimes poorly, and a few times, dismally. Even after a dark winter of trouble, I still believe a new spring will come. Sometimes I have faith that the extended personal winters will end before I too must end.

I think about Michael's younger patient who said she felt she was seventy-eight when she was only thirty-eight and remember I felt exactly that way in my thirties. Even though we have not met, I think of her especially, as I summarize my feelings and conclude my portion of our dialogue. I so want her to have many more healthy days than sick ones. Despite our obvious age difference, I want us both to arrive at the actual age of seventy-eight with considerable comfort, unable to recall vividly the thirty-eight year old women we both once were, trapped inside our bodies screaming with pain. Bodies which hardly felt like bodies at all—and certainly not ones belonging to youthful women.

If we pray, we pray for ourselves, and our families. If we have been at this long enough, as I have, it is impossible to think of ourselves without also thinking about the rest of the citizens in "our land." I want to express gratitude to friends who have stayed on with me, and find forgiveness for those who could not. I have one new serious goal since we began this collaboration: I want to comprehend in fuller terms what it is like to be a doctor of a population of patients who never really get well, and whose conditions are not easily diagnosed.

Not every story has a Hollywood ending. I wish mine did, for myself, and for all our readers who are also ill, as well as the families and friends who are involved. I know Michael wishes it for me and for all his patients, and for the millions he will never see and never get to treat. He does, in his quiet, serious, precise and intellectual way, believe all of us deserve at least a few Hollywood matinee moments. My disease still lurks and lingers. It shows up and demands attention at the most inappropriate times. My illness still transports me to the deepest abyss, sometimes quickly. When I hit the bottom, sometimes I want to turn on my brain's pre-programmed exit tape. I think again I will leave immediately on my own terms. Then, I catch my actual, my emotional breath, and say "no, not yet."

Recurrences can have a ferocious new energy, as if all the disease needed was a quick nap to regain control. These are the times when Michael teaches me again the crucial lesson to survival—I am unable to control the course of the disease or its outcome, but I do possess the power to control my responses and my reactions. When I can't summon up enough courage, I forgive myself for my sadness. I continue to work for détente with "the Rot." I suppose I always will do so. Yet, my enemy is always with me even if I can't see it or feel it. As research and medical explorations continue, and as the electronic age has made communication between doctors and patients more immediate, there is a far more optimistic future than the one I unsuspectingly awoke to one pre-teenage morning. My core identity has been kept in one piece because I have had the opportunity to be treated by a doctor who has seen the person first, and never only the disease.

This, more than any other factor, has been the key to the health of my soul, and defining essence. The doctors who are able to discern the symptom as the manifestation of a disease, as something separate from the person, help sick people more than they realize. Perhaps this book will help doctors appreciate this integral role in our lives in ways that combine both their medical knowledge and treatment decisions. I hope that in this one patient's voice, doctors of the chronically ill can hear the voices of gratitude from millions of us who have been their patients.

I did not tell the man I once loved who assigned me to "another planet" I had believed his feelings were authentic. Although I was convinced when he had said, "I am not like the others. Your illness and you do not scare me." I did not confess that trusting him was a comfort to me. I did not reveal the extent of the joy I felt when in his company, albeit for far too brief a time.

I did not tell him these things, because he was a person. He was not a place. I should not have anchored myself to his words and actions, thinking I had docked in a safe harbor. I should have anchored myself to my own strength, not in the belief in someone else's statements. When I had told him I wasn't myself when I was so ill, it was actually untrue. The truth is that being sick is also a part of me.

During the times of sickness and in wellness also, I recall those brief moments over the course of my lifetime when I shared both my love and my illness with someone. However wretched his departure made me feel, I wasn't the only person in the picture. It wasn't a one-way proposition. Of course, it never is. I am still trying to come to terms with this cosmic joke: why would any sane person volunteer to make an intimate connection with me? I try to comprehend what serious chronic illness in someone you care about might feel like for the other person.

In writing this book I have learned with a stubborn resistance that it is possible to find strength in the acceptance of alone-ness. It is by surrendering to the reality of chronic disease as a brutally isolating experience that I have found strange solace. There isn't a partner, friend, lover, companion, husband or physician who can fill that void. Only I can work at that task. I am far from conquering it, but I have yet to give up.

Some years ago, I wrote a poem for one of my dearest friends. It is entitled *All the Rivers*, and concludes with these lines:

> Don't push the river, it flows by itself,
> it flows above us, and beneath us,
> but in the middle, we dance in the moonlight
> —at the river's edge.

When I wrote the poem, I thought of the river as a metaphor for relationships. It was a poem about love's price and women's endurance. It was not a poem about chronic illness, or was it? Reading it again, I wonder whether that river represented then, as it surely does now, chronic disease itself.

Somehow, each one of us finds her own place, in the middle of our flawed and disrupted lives, to dance in the moonlight at the edge of that river. We are inside a country we did not ask to inhabit, and must tolerate much that we would never choose, but we can dance, and find more rivers to explore. We can choose to fill our world with the promise of happiness, independence and achievements. We gather more stories on our way and dream extraordinary dreams—some just might transform themselves into real experiences—providing more pieces for the jigsaw puzzle of life. When the pieces are locked together they ultimately reveal a full picture of the unchosen life as one filled with surprises, joys—and always the abiding hope that each night the moon will find our battered bodies, bathe us in her healing light, and extend us into the next day and beyond.

As I was making final revisions and edits on this book, I pushed aside many warning signals, and found myself deep in an ugly and muddy ditch, not a river, before I stopped hiding out from Michael, the doctor, as opposed to Michael, the colleague and co-author. I was afraid more than I was in denial. Some symptoms were new and profoundly painful. Others were all too familiar. But, he heeded these warning signs and put me right away in the hospital. The day I had to be admitted as an emergency case we were in the middle of a monsoon. My neighbors helped me into the lobby of my building. My friend was in her car in front, waiting to drive me to the hospital. I got out of the car at the entrance to the hospital and hugged and thanked her. I proceeded to Admitting. I spoke to the receptionist, who has been at the hospital over thirty years, and has assisted me through all my admissions. Checking in is no longer fraught with anxiety or fear.

There is fatigue, but now it is the fatigue of acceptance as much as the weariness of battle. It has become acceptable to be chronically ill. I'm not a young woman any longer. Baby boomers have health issues, and I am a baby boomer. The fact that this has been a dominant part of my entire life is not obvious or apparent to the onlooker in a hospital setting. I had all my paperwork in order. Durable medical power of attorney. Advance directives. Insurance card. I prefer to check in alone; it is less traumatic for me than for those who would willingly volunteer to come with me. My throat catches only once in the process. The admitting officer of the hospital asks me, "Next of kin, in case of emergency?" I am absolutely silent. She repeats the question. I ask to see the form.

I soberly and calmly review the reality of my life's circumstances. I write on the form: "In case of death, notify my estate lawyer," and write in his address and phone number. My lawyer is the practical answer. Hospitals need pragmatic patients. I want to be one. I force myself to move quickly beyond "what if" to other thoughts. Going upstairs to my room is no longer foreign to me or at all frightening. I know the drill. All around me I see faces I recognize. I jokingly always refer to "Michael's hospital" as my "Special Spa."

The disease is unpredictable, fierce and, at present, angry and in a fighting frame of mind. However, I know how to be a decent patient. I know what a responsible pattern of behaviors is and it is a predictable pattern for me and one I will follow. I hope something can be done to get me out of a sudden patch of severe suffering and pain I can't endure—when I thought there was not a pain I could not beat back by force of will.

I surprise myself by agreeing immediately, with no desire for negotiation, to undergo a previously untried treatment. And further shock myself by secretly and fervently praying . for a respite if not a remission.

More than anything else, I find that there has been a tremendous change in how I am regarded as the patient named Alida Brill. The world has changed. Even as I have remained an unwell woman, our world, the world of women, and for women, is not the one in which I began. More than one half of the attending house physicians taking care of me now are young women, who were all born in 1975 or later. When they ask me what I do, these doctors do not automatically assume my whole life has been sidelined by disease. They all presume I have had some sort of professional life. I tell them I write non-fiction, but leave it vague.

In the following days, I learned each one of these young doctors had "Googled" me, and learned about this book; but they also found out who I was in the world apart from my hospitalizations. They read about my work on the lives and rights of women and girls, and about my activism. Two of them thanked me for "being out there" for women so that they could become doctors. They engaged me in debate about how hard it was to become a doctor and still be a wife, a companion, a partner, and a mother. They talked carefully but in serious terms about the attitudes of some male doctors. At times, I felt as if I were running a women's history seminar and a discourse on the triumphs and failures of the feminist movement from my hospital bed; I did not at all feel like a chronically sick person.

A young resident and I talked about her life and her work, which would take her to a specialty other than rheumatology.

She complimented me on the fact that I was wearing a matching nightgown and robe, and that it was a very pretty color. I told her in a motherly and somewhat superior tone that it was important for ill women to maintain a sense of beauty, no matter the situation. She said she knew that.

Her next sentences put me back into the place I belonged, one of humility and respect, rather than the arrogance of age and survival. She explained how her mother, who had died some years before she had gone to medical school, had taught her that. She had been ill for more than a decade but never lost her identity or her sense of herself. The doctor without a mother. The patient without a daughter.

At one point an attending physician born in 1975—the year I had been both busy being ill and working for women's rights—came to see me. It was a Friday night after nine p.m. From her wedding rings, I knew she was married. She was a fellow in a competitive discipline and held a prized position. She stopped by on her way home to check on me. I was not her primary patient and it was above and beyond her duties, especially considering that she had been one of the participating doctors in an extremely painful procedure on me earlier in the day. I asked if she had any children. She had one, a son—just eighteen months old, home and asleep with her husband who was acting as the parent on duty.

We talked only briefly about my health. She accorded me the respect of someone who had not succumbed emotionally or physically to an atypical form of a confounding and nasty disease. She asked if I had a hypothesis about what might be happening to me. She had done her homework, and, although I had only met her two days before, was very familiar with my medical history. She said it looked to her like I was going through what I always went through. "Never clear or obvious with me," I said, and she nodded with agreement. Halfway out the door, she turned and came back.

"My kid is already asleep, so I might as well stay a few more minutes. You know, I have a bone to pick with you. And with my mom, and with your whole generation. You made us believe we could have it all, big careers, marriage, children. But you lied to us."

I laughed but I knew what she was feeling. My generation had helped take down the barriers, but we did not fully understand the institutional resistance that would remain for women and the extra obstacles for those who were also mothers. We pretended we knew that it would be difficult, but we didn't fully comprehend the whole thing. How could we? I looked in her eyes and saw a great deal about the meaning of women, work and equality. I said to her, "We didn't actually lie to you. We just didn't understand it all. We all have more work to do."

She suggested I should get well and do some more work. I found myself saying something I had no intention of saying because I didn't know I felt it. I told her that my next book was going to be about my experience of "becoming a woman in a time of change and confusion." I said I had thought about having a chapter that was a dialogue with her generation and asked if I could I interview her later. I wanted to interview women such as she who were born in 1975, the year that had been such a significant one for me on every front; on the barricades, in my personal life, and in hospital beds. This young doctor saw me as a writer, with work still to do, fights still to wage and lessons to learn from all the daughters I might have had, but didn't or couldn't. What Michael had seen so many years before (three decades) was what she saw also; a person, not a disease.

To these young women doctors, I was more an intriguing piece of feminist history than merely a curious set of symptoms or a bizarre case of autoimmune phenomenon. Although the disease had once again taken control of my body, it was not even close to taking a nibble out of my identity, even in that hospital setting. The big difference is that, at last, I understood that clearly too.

Previously I had found my voice as an advocate for change for women and girls. I had found my voice for women's rights to be seen and defined as civil rights. I had been published as a social critic and a writer, a champion for equality, tolerance and freedom for all people. I had retraced my childhood and written some about that journey. I had written and spoken about the corrosiveness of entrenched attitudes of sexism and prejudice. As I am no longer a young woman approaching thirty, but almost twice that age, I acknowledge much of my life has already been decided. Some were decisions I made knowingly, if in error, others I put off until it was too late to rethink them. I will never be anyone's mother, or grandmother. And, for efficiency's sake, I will probably continue to list my lawyer as the next of kin.

I end this book where I began my life—as a girl, and then as a woman—I am someone who will always be chronically ill. Thirty years ago, in the same hospital, I observed male doctors who were compassionate and concerned about a young woman undergoing the ordeal of accepting a devastating diagnosis and its aftermath. But the drama this time, my most recent hospitalization, was not about me; it was about the enormous changes that have taken place in my lifetime. The faces of women doctors surrounding me when things got rough or upsetting provided me a sense of comfort and peace I could not have predicted. It also gave me a feeling of indescribable personal pride. I have lived to tell my story to these doctors, and in turn to hear their stories and learn from them. I have engaged in a stimulating, exciting and illuminating collaboration with my physician—something I could not have imagined or conceived possible several years ago.

My last full day in the hospital, the resident who told me her mother taught her how to be sick and remain a whole woman came to check on me. As it was a holiday and the hospital was fairly quiet, she had time to chat. I asked about her plans and the years ahead of her, which included an upcoming marriage. We talked about balancing lives and the differences in the world I knew at twenty-seven compared to the one she knew at twenty-seven. Then, with a sweetly sly smile she said to me, "Someday, maybe you will Google me too." I tugged on her white coat, maintaining respect for her status as a physician, but admittedly with a bit of a maternal attitude, and replied, "You are going to have an ascendant career. I promise you."

And we said good-bye. There it was, not exactly the last piece of the jigsaw puzzle, but an important one. All these pieces of my life, the sick life and the well life, the life of this one woman and the people that have touched me and healed me and that I have touched and perhaps healed in different kinds of ways—all of them interlocking with one another. The completed puzzle is one portraying a life lived with disease in it, but not of disease alone.

It is not the life I would have chosen…

But it is my very own life, and even if it is not one with a traditional Hollywood ending, it is one with enough satisfaction to keep me going forward. There will be days and weeks, or at least, moments of wellness, and there will continue to be sequences of illness, episodes of good and bad, but each will contain its share of happy experiences and encounters.

Like I said…it really hasn't been all bad.

AB

I Am Me

It is easy, I suppose, when you are a very young doctor, an intern or resident, or if you only deal with hospitalized patients to see them only as faceless figures in hospital gowns. You ignore the pictures on the bedside stand, the visitors who come and go, the taped-to-the-wall, crayoned get-well pictures from the youngest members of the clan, and cease to know these people, whose existences are momentarily under your control; you think of them only in terms of their body parts that have failed or in what room order you will encounter them on your daily rounds. If you are a hospital physician it is easy to think that you are the center of these peoples' lives.

But you are not. I often remind young doctors (and, I am sure, am sneered at for my pomposity in return) that a year from now "the pneumonia in 202-B" or "the coronary down the hall" will not remember the intern's and resident's names, may have pushed this hospital experience to the back of her mind, and will have returned to an existence that they know little of.

Doctors who treat patients with chronic illness are more aware than, I suppose, many of their acute-care colleagues, that patients come wrapped not only in clothes (a particularly attractive color, a new hair style, a new engagement ring) but also in life experiences (a new book just released, a one-person show about to open, an exciting trip, a move, a job, a thrilling or devastating personal event about to occur) and families (a sib or parent or child's illness, an estrangement or a reconciliation or a birth)—personal trappings that to them carry far more import than does the visit they pay to you today. Is a new prescription needed? If so, its purpose is only partly to make the patient feel better. Mostly, feeling better is a secondary goal for the patient; she wants to feel better so that she can get on with her life.

To chronic disease physicians and their patients, hospitalizations are intermittent, disruptive, but also transient, fleeting events, momentary deviations from a trajectory. Or, I should say, two trajectories, parallel, or perhaps more precisely, like DNA, intertwined and twisted into a helix, one strand the path of the disease, the other the path of the patient's life, both playing out in her *katun*.

In the worst circumstances the two trajectories are more like binary stars, the motion of one obligating motion of the other. In better—one hopes in most—times, the influence of illness is more subtle, like one of those hidden bodies of matter or energy in deep space, the existence of which can be inferred only because of a subtle bending of light. The personal trajectories of most people with chronic illness deviate only slightly from the projected path. Only non-physicians whose tools are extremely refined, and whose training is sufficiently skilled, and the doctors, who are given special permission to enter this world, will ever see the small differences that distinguish one trajectory from the other, between what is, and what might have been.

I oversimplify, of course. It is hard to trivialize the outside force when one's temperature is 104 degrees, when joints hurt so much that one cannot rise from bed, when kidneys fail, or when one has had a stroke. Those points matter in the short term, but less so when the trajectory is measured in years. Even so, when the external force seems overwhelming, when the trajectory appears to be making a U-turn, I remain astounded by the strengths of patients' personalities and by the force with which they continue to declaim: "I am still me!"

The day before I wrote this, one of our trainees asked me

to see a patient with her, a patient new to us, a young woman in her early twenties, who, the trainee thought, was seriously ill. The patient had been under treatment elsewhere and had come to our clinic to ask us to rethink her care. To the trainee, the young lady was very sick. She suffered from both sickle cell anemia and severe, devastating, long-standing, systemic lupus erythematosus.

When I entered the room I saw her lying on the examining bed, a noteworthy point, since the trainee and I had been conversing in my office for ten minutes or more; a less sick patient would have sat on the bed or on a chair in the room. She looked exhausted. She was covered from head to toe with a horribly disfiguring rash, the kind that makes people in subways shy away, and she was nearly bald as a result of her disease. I saw at a glance that she was breathing rapidly and that her heart was racing—neither of which are encouraging signs.

This consultation occurred on a Friday afternoon before a holiday weekend. It would be difficult to do an expeditious evaluation in the outpatient department. Pre-holiday Friday afternoons are the same no matter what business you are in.

"Come into the hospital," I suggested, "so we can rapidly find out what is wrong and initiate treatment to help."

"No," she replied. I have friends to see and appointments to keep. I have been this ill before, and I know what to do. I can wait, I can do this as an outpatient, she said, and (she didn't say) I will live my own life as I wish to do. She made jokes about the wigs she owned and the make-up she used to cover the rash. I can handle this, she, in effect, told us. I am me! I have my own life to live! The disease is not me!

A few weeks ago a man in New York, standing beside a subway track, had an epileptic seizure and fell in front of an oncoming train. A bystander leaped onto the track, grabbed the young man, pulled him between the two rails, covered the unconscious man's body with his own as the train rolled above their heads, and both survived without harm. Everyone— the mayor, the press— called the bystander a hero. Even the President of the United States presented him in person in a feel-good moment at the State of the Union address the week after.

In my office a few days later I talked to a young lawyer patient of mine who commented in passing—one of those messages I had once been unable to hear—how hard it was for her not to show the pain she had every day, in her office, and how hard it was to continue to produce good work when her illness left her exhausted all the time.

The bystander who leaped onto the track, I thought, is not the only hero. The real heroes are those patients of mine, like this woman, who endure and endure and yet continue to achieve. Most of us lead lives that have small troubles and small pleasures, and we complain and we smile and we expect that this is the way it should be. My heroes, my patients, lead just as fulfilling lives and also experience those troubles and pleasures—while carrying an encumbrance that none of the rest of us, those who have our health, can possibly imagine.

It is fashionable nowadays to be shocked to learn that a world-class athlete has used strength-enhancing drugs to get to the place he is in order to compete. Consider the same issue this way: what if the athlete won the race, or even finished the race, weighed down by a disability of any kind you choose? This is what my patients do every day. They run their races not enhanced, but weighed down. No one lauds them for this. Quite the contrary, often they are told: you can't be so sick. Look what you can do. These people, not the subway bystander, are true heroes, but they do not get praise. At best they get the internal satisfaction of succeeding in what is really important in their lives, to be able to proclaim: I am me!

And what magnificent feats they achieve! It would be exhausting to list all those that I have seen, but let me share a few examples. Alida, of course. Look at the biography of her "other" life. Another patient, also a young lawyer, was transferred to our hospital having just suffered a major stroke—at age twenty-eight! It was particularly hard for me to see this patient. She is quite beautiful and quite accomplished. She is a doctor's child. I have a daughter about her age, also a lawyer (also beautiful, also accomplished). It is hard for me not to imagine the girl as my daughter, or myself in her father's place. I felt self-conscious anguish every time I entered her hospital room. When I first met her, this young lady had completely lost her ability to speak, and was completely paralyzed on her right side.

That was five years ago. She now speaks well again, in at least two languages, that I am aware. She walks with a decided limp. Spasms of a paralyzed arm and leg cause her considerable pain. Notwithstanding her disability, she founded an international consulting company that manages legal aspects of technology transfer. She travels worldwide. She remains almost surrealistically cheerful. She is even dating again. She had a setback this past year for which I had to hospitalize her again, and had to prescribe medications that have very unpleasant side effects. Still, she healed rapidly, retained her cheer (or the cheerful part of her personality that she allows me to see) and resumed the (slightly altered) trajectory that is rightly hers. There is this bit of hidden dark force out there, whose gravity drags her down ever so slightly as she proceeds on her personal path, causing it to deviate a small amount, imperceptible to all but those of us who know, but this lady will not be stopped. The disease will not define her. The disease is certainly not her.

The disease is not me! This affirmation applies to most of my patients. My co-author is not, and has never been, "a Wegener's." She is Alida. She is a friend and a neighbor, a writer, a thinker, an adviser, who carries a private burden that is hidden to most of the outside world. I have the technical training first to see and then to ameliorate at least some of the distress; thus, I'm permitted a glimpse into this otherwise secret part.

To the best I can, I compartmentalize, doing the technical things that I need to do when I need to be a doctor, keeping the personal out of it or, as with the doctor's daughter, trying to hide what I personally feel when it intrudes, while knowing that beneath the illness—strike that…above the illness!—there exists a real person, who has a life and is full of ambitions, for whom illness is an underlying fact, albeit an inconvenient fact, but only a fact, far removed from the person that she knows herself to be.

MDL

Acknowledgments

My primary debt is to Michael Lockshin, M.D. whose vision for the treatment of chronically ill people is a model unto itself, and its own kind of miracle.

I am grateful, beyond measure, to the staff, medical and administrative at Hospital for Special Surgery and New York Hospital. —And especially to everyone at the Barbara Volcker Center for Women and Rheumatic Disease and the entire team in the Infusion Room.

With particular appreciation to Renata Ochabski, M.D., whose judgment averted an ocular disaster.

Our publisher Tim Schaffner of Schaffner Press reminded me again why I chose to be a writer. His editorial wisdom, grace of spirit and of language was an author's dream as the project moved from concept to ideas to manuscript to finished book.

To Joshua Jason of JJPR—thank you for your enthusiasm, skill and faith in the stories we have told.

My beloved friends, Greta G. Pearson and Robert Pearson, have endured many episodes of illness with me. They have done so with uncommon patience and unfailing support. To Mara Robinson and Chuck Robinson, with love and deepest thanks for their friendship which makes the journey possible instead of unbearable.

Robin Morgan, my sister in the larger struggle for all women, whose friendship and relentless loyalty sustain me, and whose work and life constantly inspire and humble me.

My childhood friend, Kathe Foy Nagy, guides me through the rough passages, forcing me to laugh when everything else fails. For decades, Lani Reynolds, and Gary and Judy Karinen have held a personal safety net securely underneath me. With gratitude to the "daughters": Susan Johntz, M.D., from the first and always in my heart. Jenny Karinen stuns, amazes, and makes me happy. Kiki Foy Nagy, teacher of the important lessons. Kim H. Walls, for reasons she can't imagine. Laura Hedy Fiske, my summer daughter, who invited me to become a part of her life.

To Daliah Brill, who seems always to understand. Bernadette Bucher gave me shelter in her serene country home where portions of this book were drafted. With thanks to S.S.M. for maintaining a standard I will never attain, but in which I find affirmation and reassurance. Finally, with appreciation to my large "family of choice"—in different ways all have kept their hands on my back, gently pushing me forward: Marjorie Agosín, Anne Bloom, Brian Capon and Don Terwilliger, Patricia Conrad, M.D., Christopher Cory, Jane Isay Dolger, John Engel, Howard and Cynthia Fuchs Epstein, Janet Farnsworth, Daniel Fendel, Julian Fifer, Pamela Franklin, Michael Gutstadt, Barbara Goen, Helene Goldfarb, Florence Howe, Richard Isay, M.D., Harvey Jason, Louis Jason, Maddy Lee, Jackie Leverone and Jim Stafford, Mark Nelkin, Elizabeth Neuse, Joan and Ray Silver, Randee Trabitz, Joann Vanek, David Velinsky, Linda Wolfe, and so many others who have crossed into my life, filling it with compassion and healing. And, in blessed memory of Betty Friedan and Professor Dame Mary Douglas, my maternal "bookends."

AB

Acknowledgments

This book would not have been possible without the constant, thoughtful, and often impassioned thoughts that my patients shared with me—I learned from you all, and am humbled. I can't name you all but you know who you are. My family was unsparingly critical, and imaginative, and encouraging, and so helped shape this book from its very diffuse beginnings. My colleagues and friends at the Hospital for Special Surgery and the New York Presbyterian Hospital, nurses, administrative staff, students, and doctors have throughout the years contributed in some way by sharing their thoughts each and every day. In particular I thank my office staff, Meylin Aponte Lucena and Ansara Muntaz, the many nurses, especially Linda Leff and Natalie Morgan, our social service staff, especially Roberta Horton and Suzi Kim, and many other members of our hospital, such as Lillian Diaz-Arroyo, who have taken me aside and told me what individual patients actually thought but were afraid to talk about. Dr. Steven Paget and Mr. Paul Volcker each contributed in their way by allowing me the freedom to think beyond the day-to-day routine. Finally, Tim Schaffner had the vision to bring this project together, to edit it wisely, and to see it come to fruition.

MDL

About the Authors

Alida Brill is a feminist social critic. She has written and spoken on such diverse topics as medical and sexual privacy, the ethics surrounding the right to die, the role of gender during periods of economic transition, intolerance and prejudice, and the conflict between personal versus public politics in a democracy.

She is the author of *Nobody's Business: The Paradoxes of Privacy,* and the editor of *A Rising Public Voice: Women in Politics Worldwide.* In 1983 she was co-author, with Herbert McClosky, of the landmark book, *Dimensions of Tolerance: What Americans Believe About Civil Liberties.* Her essays and commentaries have appeared in a variety of anthologies, journals, magazines and websites.

Alida has suffered from autoimmune illness since adolescence. It was eventually diagnosed as an atypical form of Wegener's Granulamatosis. This is the first time she has chosen to chronicle her experiences about a life lived with illness.

Alida lives in New York City and is at work on a new inspirational memoir, titled *Secret Dances: Moving Above and Beyond Chronic Illness,* to be published in 2011. Visit her website at www.alidabrill.com.

Michael Lockshin, M.D. is one of the world's leading experts in the long-term care of chronically ill patients. He is the Director of the Barbara Volcker Center for Women and Rheumatic Disease at the Hospital for Special Surgery in New York City and a professor of medicine and obstetrics/gynecology at the Weill Medical College of Cornell University.

He serves as Editor-in-Chief of "Arthritis & Rheumatism," the official publication of the American College of Rheumatology, and his books for the general reader include *Guarded Prognosis: A Doctor and His Patients Talk About Chronic Disease and How to Cope With It,* and (as co-author) *The Hospital for Special Surgery Rheumatoid Arthritis Handbook.* He and his wife Jane live in New York. To find out more, visit: www.michaellockshin.com.

About the Publisher

Schaffner Press is an independent publisher dedicated to books of quality in non-fiction and fiction that deal with topics of universal import and concern to the general reader. To learn more about Schaffner Press. visit:www.schaffnerpress.com